THE INTERNATIONAL
VEGETARIAN
COOKBOOK

THE INTERNATIONAL
VEGETARIAN
COOKBOOK

Kirsten Skaarup

GARDEN WAY PUBLISHING
POWNAL, VERMONT 05261

Illustrations by Sheila MacMahon
Cover design and illustration by Ken Braren and Loretta Trezzo

Editor: Roger Griffith
Translated by Bodil Wilson

Copyright 1982 by Kirsten Skaarup and Høst & Søns Forlag, Copenhagen, entitled Vegtarisk Køkken.

Published in the United States 1984 by Storey Communications, Inc., Pownal, Vermont 05261

The name Garden Way Publishing has been licensed to Storey Communications, Inc., by Garden Way, Inc.

Printed in the United States
Printing (last digit): 10 9 8 7 6 5 4 3 2 1

Library of Congress Cataloging in Publication Data
Skaarup, Kirsten.
  The international vegetarian cookbook.

  Translation of: Vegtarisk kokken.
  Includes index.
  1. Vegetarian cookery.   2. Cookery, International.
I. Title.
TX837.S5313   1983   641.5'636   83-25318
ISBN 0-88266-362-3 (pbk.)

CONTENTS

FOREWORD · vii

AN INTRODUCTION
TO VEGETARIAN COOKING · 1

THE VEGETARIAN PANTRY · 5

HERBS & FLAVORINGS · 17

SPROUTS · 20

LACTIC ACID FERMENTATION · 22

SEITAN · 25

UTENSILS · 27

HANDLING VEGETABLES · 28

BREAKFAST · 29

LUNCH · 32

SALADS · 35

SOUPS · 53

FIRST COURSES · 67

MAIN COURSES · 80

A FRAGRANCE FROM THE EAST · 110

PÂTÉS & RISSOLES · 118

FESTIVE GREEN FOODS · 124

SAUCES & ACCOMPANIMENTS · 136

DESSERTS · 159

BAKING · 166

INDEX · 176

FOREWORD

For years I have carried on in my mind a losing debate with vegetarians and their thoughts on a sane diet for Americans.

Yes, I agree, Americans do overeat. We see proof of this on every beach. They don't need all that protein, that fat, that sugar, and they carry with them, in fleshy bulges, the evidence to prove it.

And, yes, there is simply no sense in a world food production and distribution system that raises food for animals so that a relatively few of us can eat meat, when that same land could provide food—more than enough—for people who are starving today. It's alarming, too, I agree, when we see those in other nations moving in our direction toward a meat-centered diet.

I will concede, also, that vegetarians are healthier than meat-eaters. It is not the considerable weight of the statistics that convinces me, but the lean look, the flow of health I see on the faces of those who say "no" when the meat platter is passed. This is a most difficult concession for those of us who since childhood have learned to equate meat and potatoes with strength and vigor and good health.

Finally, I agree, of course, that the grocery bill could be cut beautifully if that item, "meat for tonight and Sunday," were crossed off the grocery list before we reached the supermarket.

Then why, you ask, why is meat so important to you? Why, when the moral, finanacial, health, and all other arguments say to go in the other direction?

My answer is a simple one.

It's necessary to fuel this body of mine with food. It can be done just about that mechanically, or that thrice-daily refueling can be a delightful experience, particularly when each meal is carefully planned, artfully cooked, pleasingly served.

In contrast, I recall one vegetarian cookbook in which recipes begin, with depressing and monotonous regularity, "Heat oil in a skillet and sauté the garlic. . . ."

And another in which brewer's yeast, bran, and wheat germ were featured in endless combinations cool to the tongue, dismal to the taste.

The sacrifice, I concluded was too great to give up a daily pleasure for a diet that offered refueling but little more.

And then . . .

But of course you knew how this would come out. I met Kirsten Skaarup, I read the translation of her book, I sampled those recipes, the best of international vegetarian cuisine. My eyes were opened. I was convinced.

Vegetarian cooking is not just a way to healthier living or an act of protest against the international food system.

No, it's far more than that. It's an opportunity to experience new pleasures in eating, to savor delicate combinations of vegetables, the richness of grains. It's an opportunity for many to go from the dullness of today's pre-prepared and prepackaged foods to meals that are delicious as well as a delight to the eye.

I hope you will share this pleasure with me as you read and try Kirsten's many recipes. We agree with Kirsten that a change in eating habits can be the first step toward a healthier lifestyle for you and your family.

M. John Storey
Publisher

INTRODUCTION

While it is not necessary to make a comprehensive study of the laws of nutrition in order to eat properly, it might be beneficial for you to read for a moment what makes the body function.

Energy

Just as a motor needs fuel, the body also requires fuel for energy.

Energy is derived from food and is utilized when proteins, fats, and carbohydrates are burned up by the body.

How much energy you require depends on your level of activity, age, sex, and other factors. If your body is supplied more fuel than it burns, the excess is stored as fat.

Protein

The properly varied vegetarian diet will almost automatically meet the body's need for the necessary vitamins and minerals. If, in addition, milk products and eggs are consumed, the body's requirement for protein will also be met.

The fear that vegetarians suffer from protein deficiency is completely unfounded. There is no doubt that people in the West get sick more often from eating too much rather than too little protein-rich food.

In the United States, the National Academy of Sciences estimates that the daily requirement of protein is 56 grams for a 154-pound male, or about .8 grams per kilogram of weight, and 44 grams for a 128-pound woman, or about .75 grams per kilogram of weight. The question is whether this is more protein than is required. Whether one is just a plain vegetarian or an ovo-lacto-vegetarian—allowing oneself a few milk products and eggs—there is good reason to take a closer look at the question of proteins.

The proteins are made up of 22 different amino acids, most of which are produced by the body itself. Eight of them, the so-called essential, even life-essential, amino acids must be supplied through nutritional intake on a daily basis. These essential amino acids are: phenylalanine, isoleucine, leucine, lysine, methionine, threonine, tryptophan, and valine.

The biological value of various proteins is measured according to the organism's ability to use them. The biologically valuable proteins, then, are those with a composition of amino acids that best satisfy the body's requirements.

This means that the different proteins do not have equal biological value. If only one of the essential amino acids is missing, it will affect the whole protein utilization process, and it matters not that all the other amino acids are present in the required amounts.

In general, the proteins of vegetable products have less

biological value than those of animal products. The vegetarian's food must, therefore, be so composed that the amino acids properly complement each other.

For example, grain products hold a low content of lysine, whereas leafy vegetables and legumes have a large lysine content.

The methionine content of legumes and vegetables is low, whereas methionine is plentiful in nuts and seeds.

By properly combining foods with low biological values, it is possible to obtain foods with high biological value.

In addition to the foods already mentioned, the amino acids may be balanced with combinations like the following to provide the proper amino acids.

Beans + buckwheat + millet + vegetables
Rice + beans or peas + leafy vegetables
Potatoes + milk + vegetables
Rice + green vegetables + nuts
Beans + sesame seeds + green vegetables
Grain products + green vegetables + sesame seeds
Grain products + milk (possibly) + beans
Green vegetables + milk + sesame seeds
Potatoes + eggs
Potatoes + grain products

Oils and Fats

Fatty substances consist mainly of saturated, unsaturated, and polyunsaturated fatty acids. Most of the fatty substances contain all three kinds of fatty acids in varying amounts. The polyunsaturated fatty acids lower the blood cholesterol level, whereas saturated fatty acids raise it.

Much of the unsaturated and polyunsaturated fatty acids are found mainly in vegetable oils such as corn oil, sunflower oil, soybean oil, as well as in safflower oil, nuts, almonds, and grain products.

Fatty substances in animal products are mainly the saturated fatty acids.

The vegetarian kitchen uses mainly vegetable oils when preparing foods.

Carbohydrates

The carbohydrates in food consist of starch and sugar. Starch is converted into glucose (blood sugar), and is either burned and turned into energy, or stored in the liver and muscles.

The good carbohydrates, which are broken down slowly, are obtained from grain products, potatoes, and other vegetables. The carbohydrates in fruits are also beneficial, although assimilated more rapidly.

The less beneficial carbohydrates are contained in refined sugar and sugar products such as brown sugar and syrup, as well as in white flour. When sugars are consumed, the blood sugar level is raised rapidly, and the body is forced to work extra hard in order to increase the insulin production. In addition, sugar causes a quick formation of fat.

Cellulose cannot be broken down in the body. It consists of hard particles, shells, and fibers from vegetables and grains.

Fiber-rich foods have several advantages. The fibers are instrumental in maintaining a good digestive system, thereby preventing many diseases common to the present-day civilization. In addition, research indicates that fiber-rich foods are of great importance in weight loss control. The fibers are filling and satisfy hunger pains. Foods rich in fibers include potatoes, beans, and grains.

Vitamins

Vitamins are organic substances which in many ways transform the nutritional intake and control the mineral content of the body. Thus, lack of any single vitamin may indicate that the body will be unable to absorb one or more minerals and thereby cause an imbalance.

There are two kinds of vitamins, the fat-soluble and the water-soluble vitamins. The fat-soluble vitamins are vitamins A, D, E, and K. An excess of these can be stored in the body.

The water-soluble vitamins are the B vitamins and vitamin C. Excess intake of these vitamins is excreted through the urine, and they must therefore be taken on a daily basis with food.

In a varied vegetarian diet, which includes fresh vegetables and the water in which they are boiled, lack of vitamins is not likely to be a risk.

Some vegetarians are afraid they may lack vitamin B12, but the daily need of this vitamin can be met by drinking a pint of milk.

Minerals and Trace Minerals

Minerals and trace minerals are non-organic substances that are needed to build and maintain body health. The body does not manufacture its own minerals; these, therefore, must be supplied continually. The cells and the metabolism will only function normally if the correct amount of minerals and trace minerals is added to the diet.

The need for minerals varies. Most important are calcium, phosphorus, iron, sodium, and potassium. Other important minerals are iodine, magnesium, manganese, zinc, copper, silicic acid, and fluorine. The body needs only very small amounts of the trace minerals selenium, mercury, cobalt, chromium, lead, tin, silver, gold, and molybdenum.

If your diet contains many refined products from very exhausted soil, there is probably reason to supplement it with minerals.

Acid-Alkaline Balance

What we eat has either an acid or an alkaline forming effect. The alkaline-producing products are most vegetables, fruits, berries—both fresh and dried—as well as milk and curdled milk products.

Acid-producing products are meats and fish, eggs and cheese, all grain products, legumes, butter, cream, and other fatty substances.

If one eats too many acid-producing products, the eliminating organs, lungs, kidneys, and skin will be overloaded. If the overload is so great that they cannot handle it, the excess acid is stored in the body, and this may cause various diseases, such as arthritis and decreased resistance to infections.

A nutrition researcher who has gone into the phenomenon of the acid-base balance, is Dr. Ragnar Berg of Sweden, who contends that a well-balanced diet should consist of 70–80 percent alkaline and 20–30 percent acid-forming foods.

THE VEGETARIAN PANTRY

Vegetarians eat many foods with which non-vegetarians may be unfamiliar. The following list of the most common products, their use and nutritional value, is meant as an aid to their better utilization.

Vegetables are not included in the list, since the recipes use mainly the ordinary, well-known vegetables. In the few cases where newer or less-known vegetables are used, they will be described in connection with one of the recipes in which they are used.

Agar-agar. See seaweed.

Arrowroot. See kuzo.

Beans, Lentils, and Dried Peas (Legumes) are rich in proteins, carbohydrates, vitamins (especially the B vita-

mins), and the minerals iron, calcium, and phosphorus. Vitamin C is created when the legumes sprout. Legumes, with the exception of the yellow soybean, do not contain all of the essential amino acids; they should therefore be supplemented with rice, grain products (wheat, among others), and vegetables. Rice and grain products should be soaked in water, then cooked with the legumes.

Legumes are very nutritious, but are not easily digested, so should be included only sparingly in the diet. They can be used in soups, salads, main courses, pâtés, and with meat balls, or they can be used as a side dish. They mix well with garlic and most spices.

Beans are also used for sprouting.

Before being cooked, beans and peas should be soaked in water for at least 8 hours. Remember that they will swell with soaking.

Legumes are cooked for 30 to 90 minutes in the water in which they have been soaked. Salt may be added during the last 10 minutes of cooking. If you add a little lemon juice or apple cider vinegar, the cooking time can be shortened. The water in which the legumes are cooked should be discarded, as some of the legumes give off purine (the parent of uric acid) while cooking. You can also change the water when the legumes are half-cooked.

Keep an eye on the beans during cooking, as they will turn mealy if they are overcooked.

Soybeans are the richest in protein but also the most indigestible of the bean family. They must be cooked for 1½ hours.

Green mung beans are easier to digest. Therefore, they need to be soaked only for a couple of hours and cooked for about 30 to 40 minutes. *Azuki beans* are cooked for 50 to 60 minutes. *Red kidney beans* and *black-eyed peas* are cooked for about 45 minutes. *Pinto, lima,* and *garbanzo beans* are cooked for about 1 hour. *Broad beans (fava beans)* are big and flat. They should be cooked for about 30 minutes. *Yellow* and *green dried peas* are cooked a little more than 1 hour. *Lentils* are either green, red, or dark (*French lentils*). They do not need any pre-soaking and are cooked for about 30 minutes.

Buckwheat. See grain products.

Bulgur. See grain products.

Cheese is rich in protein and contains vitamins A and B.

Rennet is used in the manufacturing of most cheeses, except cream cheese. This is an animal enzyme. If you want to avoid this, health food stores sell hard cheeses, such as cheddar, double Gloucester, and red Leicester, which are manufactured with vegetable enzymes.

Couscous. See grain products.

Dried Fruits have a considerably greater nutritional value than fresh fruits, but they are also richer in carbohydrates. Buy the unsulphured dried fruits in the health food stores.

Dried fruits are soaked for a couple of hours prior to use. They may be used for breakfast, in salads, side dishes, main courses, desserts, and cakes.

The most common kinds are prunes, figs, dates, raisins, apricots, bananas, apples, and pears.

In addition, one may get dried chestnuts, which are very easy to handle as they are already peeled. The dried chestnuts are soaked for about 8 hours before use and are cooked until soft (about 15 minutes) in the water in which they were soaked.

Dried mushrooms are soaked for a couple of hours before use and must be cleaned very thoroughly, since they are very often full of soil and sand.

When the mushrooms have been soaked enough, they are treated like fresh mushrooms.

Eggs. In the vegetarian kitchen eggs are usually used very sparingly, but eggs are very nutritious (they contain calcium, iron, and vitamins A and B), and they contain proteins with an ideal amino acid combination.

The production of eggs is now getting to be so much of a mistreatment of hens that it must be a question for each individual to answer for himself whether he wants to use eggs at all, unless he can buy fresh eggs from a farm where the hens are running free and not kept in cages for production.

Eggs may be replaced in many dishes, for instance in pâtés, by soy flour or buckwheat flour mixed with a little water.

Gomasio is a natural spice made from roasted sesame seeds and unrefined sea salt. May be used as a table salt.

Grain products make up a large part of the basic diet for many people all over the world. They play an important role in the vegetarian's diet.

Grains are, largely speaking, rich in proteins, and contain a variety of essential amino acids. The vitamin and mineral contents also vary. It is therefore a good idea to eat a variety of different grains or to mix them in cereals and breads.

When baking, it is best to grind the flour immediately prior to use.

Various kinds of grain mills and grinders are sold. The best grinding is done in a stone grinder.

Not everybody can grind his own flour. Health food stores carry whole grains as well as various kinds of ground flour.

Whole grains, which can be used as supplements or added to many courses, are soaked for 12 hours and then cooked in double the amount of water for about 1 hour.

Whole wheat contains proteins, vitamins A, B, and E, as well as calcium, sodium, potassium, phosphorus, iron, zinc, magnesium, and silicic acid. Whole wheat is used as a supplement, in cereals, and for baking.

Cracked wheat contains all the nutritional elements of whole wheat, and is used mainly for baking and for cereals.

Whole grain wheat flour contains all the nutritional elements of the whole grains. It is often mixed with white or unbleached flour for baking.

Graham flour is a finer grain than whole grain wheat flour, but it also contains all the nutrition of the whole grains. It is used for baking, mixed with white or unbleached flour.

Wheat flakes contain all of the whole grain nutrition and are used for baking and in muesli.

Wheat germ is a good source of vitamin E and contains the B vitamins as well as potassium, sodium, iron, and phosphorus. Wheat germ contains fat and should be refrigerated, otherwise it will become rancid. It is used in muesli and sprinkled on soups and bread.

Wheat bran contains phylic acid, which binds the majority of the mineral content (calcium, iron, and zinc) so that it cannot be absorbed in the body. This is not of

great importance, unless bran is used in great amounts, in which case the phylic acid may cleave, be set free. This is done by soaking the bran at least 12 hours in water with 2 tablespoons of sour milk added. Wheat bran is mostly used for baking.

White (enriched) wheat flour has been finely ground and sifted, which removes practically all of the nutritional substances. It is usually enriched with vitamins B and C as well as with calcium and iron.

Bulgur is coarse, crushed wheat kernels, usually cooked and served as a side dish. The kernels are roasted with a little oil or butter and cooked in double the amount of water for 20 to 30 minutes. They are then left to soak for another 15 minutes.

Couscous is often made of semolina, and is eaten especially in North Africa. It is cooked separately and served as a side dish. The semolina is placed in a colander, and it is steam cooked by placing the colander over the large saucepan in which the main dish is cooking.

Whole rye grains contain B vitamins, calcium, sodium, phosphorus, magnesium, fluoride, silicic acid, and iron, and are used in the same way as wheat grains.

Cracked rye, coarse rye flour, and rye flakes contain all of the nutrition contained in whole rye. The first two are used for baking and porridge; rye flakes are used for muesli and baking.

Sifted rye flour is ground grain from which the bran has been removed. Used for baking.

Whole oat grain contains proteins, B and E vitamins, calcium, sodium, potassium, iron, phosphorus, magnesium, fluoride, and silicic acid. Whole oat grains are used in the same way as whole wheat and whole rye grains.

Oat flakes may be eaten uncooked with milk. They may be used in muesli soaked in water or in dry muesli, or cooked as porridge or used in baking.

Whole barley (pearled barley) contains proteins, vitamins B and E, calcium, sodium, potassium, and silicic acid. It is used in the same way as other whole grains.

Cracked barley grains contain all the nutritional substances of whole grains. They are used for baking and porridge.

Barley flakes (rolled) contain all of the nutritional substances of the whole grains. They are used in muesli, for porridge, and for baking.

Barley flour is used for porridge and baking.

Brown rice, unhulled rice, or *natural rice,* as it is sometimes referred to in this book, is unhulled or unpolished rice. Natural rice contains proteins, vitamins B and E, and about 4 times as much iron and calcium as polished (converted) rice. In addition, it contains potassium and magnesium and is rich in phosphorus. There are several grains of rice: long, short, and round, and there is also mountain rice.

In the Scandinavian countries, rice is first and foremost used as a side dish. It is also used in some main dishes, salads, and desserts. Rice is cooked in double the amount of water for about 40 minutes.

Rice flakes are used for porridge, cooked for about 5 minutes.

Hominy grits contain proteins, the B vitamins, and only small amounts of calcium and iron, but they are high in phosphorus. Corn products are often useful for people who are allergic to other grain products. Hominy grits are used for porridge.

Cornmeal is ground corn kernels. It is used for porridge, pancakes, and for baking. It comes both coarsely and finely ground. "Maizena" flour is cornstarch. It is easily digested and is used for porridge, gruel, and for thickener.

Whole grain millet is high in silicic acid. Fifty grams of millet contain the daily requirement of iron, and 100 grams the daily requirement of fluoride. Millet also contains magnesium and phosphorus.

Whole millet is cooked either separately and served as a side dish or added to porridge, casseroles, or ground patties. Millet flakes are used for porridge and in muesli, soups, and main dishes as well as in desserts.

Whole grain buckwheat is really not a grain. It contains proteins, B vitamins, magnesium, iron, phosphorus, and potassium.

Whole grain buckwheat is used as a side dish with or in porridge and stews. Buckwheat flakes contain all the nutritional substances of whole grain buckwheat and can be added to porridge and muesli, and can be used in baking. Cracked buckwheat is either coarsely or finely ground. It contains all the nutritional substances of the whole grain buckwheat. Cracked buckwheat is used for porridge and ground patties. Buckwheat flour is used for pancakes and baking. One or two spoonfuls of buckwheat flour mixed with water may be used as a thickening agent instead of an egg.

Soy flour is ground soybeans. The flour has a high protein and fat content. It is usually mixed with other flours.

If soy flour is added to other flours, it should be in a proportion not exceeding 10 percent of the total amount of flour. Soy flour can be used in place of breadcrumbs or as an egg substitute. Use one spoonful of soy flour mixed with a little water in place of one egg as a thickening agent.

Soybean flakes are used in muesli and for baking.

Gram flour is ground garbanzo beans, used mainly in Indian dishes.

Whole meal flakes are a mixture of soybean, wheat, oats, rye, corn, and rice flakes. They have a high content of the essential amino acids and minerals. They are used in muesli or cooked for 5 to 8 minutes as porridge.

Granola is a mixture of wheat flour, oats, rolled barley, malt extract, nuts, and salt. Granola comes coarsely ground or crushed. Crushed granola may be used in place of breadcrumbs.

Kruska is a mixture of cracked oats, rye, wheat, and barley. It is used for porridge. Use 1 part grains to 4 parts water, then cook it for about 40 minutes. You can also cook it for about 5 minutes, then place the pot in a box lined with hay for a minimum of 2 hours. The old-world custom is to wrap the pot with newspapers before placing it in the box. While modern American households do not contain such old-fashioned cooking devices, the cook might improvise, using a down quilt.

Honegar contains equal portions of apple cider vinegar and honey. It is used in dressing the same as herbal vinegar.

Kruska. See grain products.

Kuzo is the crushed root of the kuzo vine, which comes from Japan. Originally kuzo was used as a herbal remedy and is said to be very effective in cases of stomach and intestinal ailments. The root is also said to have beneficial effects in case of infections.

Kuzo is used as a thickening for soups and sauces. The ground or granulated root is dissolved in water in proportions of 1 to 2 teaspoons kuzo to half cup of water. Thickening with kuzo results in a delicious and easily digested sauce.

Lentils. See legumes.

Milk Products have a high protein content and a good combination of amino acids. In addition, they contain calcium, phosphorus, and vitamins A and B. Milk products can be part of many dishes. They also complete the proteins of potatoes.

Millet. See grain products.

Miso is a paste made from fermented soybeans. To this are added grain, rice, or buckwheat, and salt. Its consistency is similar to that of peanut butter. Miso comes from the Far East, where it is one of the most important soybean products. It is rich in proteins, vitamins, and minerals, and has a multitude of uses. It can be used in soups, it makes a tasteful addition to vegetable dishes, and it may be used as a salt substitute. It should be used sparingly as it contains about 5.5 to 13 percent salt.

Miso can be purchased in health food stores. You should be sure that the miso is naturally fermented.

Mustard. Natural mustard is made from mustard seeds, apples, lemons, vegetables, and herbs.

Nuts and Seeds play a major role in the vegetarian kitchen. They have a tremendous nutritional value, containing proteins (although not all of the essential ones), vitamins, and minerals, and are high in the unsaturated

fatty acids. Nuts and seeds may be utilized in all kinds of dishes, from muesli at breakfast to the dessert in the evening. They may be used whole, slivered, chopped, or minced. Many are usually added to the food just before it is served.

Almonds contain a number of essential amino acids and minerals, such as calcium, potassium, phosphorus, and iron.

Hazelnuts are rich in calcium and contain vitamins A, B, and C.

Walnuts contain vitamins A, B, and C, plus calcium, phosphorus, and other minerals.

Brazil nuts contain B vitamins and are rich in calcium, phosphorus, and other minerals.

Peanuts contain vitamins A and B as well as potassium.

Cashew nuts contain B vitamins, iron, and phosphorus.

Coconuts are not very rich in protein, but have a reasonable mineral content, such as potassium, iron, phosphorus, and chlorine. Coconuts contain the undesirable saturated fatty acids.

Sunflower seeds contain an excellent combination of nutritional substances. In addition to proteins, vitamins, and minerals, such as silicic acid, iron, copper, and various trace minerals, they also contain important enzymes and have a high content of unsaturated fatty acids.

Pumpkin seeds have a high linolic acid content. Additionally, they contain vitamins B and E plus copper and a number of trace minerals, and they are rich in unsaturated fatty acids.

Sesame seeds are rich in minerals and contain, among other minerals, calcium, phosphorus, and magnesium.

Linseeds are consumed mainly for their helpful effect on the digestion.

Oils and Fatty Substances. The most commonly used forms of fat are butter, margarine, and oil. Since margarine is a very artificial and over-refined product, it is normally not used in the health-conscious household. Butter is a pure and natural product, but it contains mainly saturated fatty acids. Therefore, vegetable oil is preferable for cooking.

Most vegetable oils are rich in polyunsaturated fatty acids. If obtainable, pure virgin olive oil should be used. The most beneficial way of extracting oil is by cold pressing. Cold-pressed oils retain both nutrients and taste. In addition to olive oil, you may now also purchase cold-pressed corn oil, sunflower oil, and sesame oil.

No matter which form of oil is used, it should be only in moderate amounts. If the recipes do not call for a specified amount of oil, as for example for sautéing, it means that as little as possible should be used. Olive oil, walnut oil, corn oil, and safflower oil are mainly used for sautéing.

For salad dressings, you may use corn oil, sunflower oil, safflower oil, or soy oil. These oils have a rich content of the life-essential linolic acid.

For buttering sandwiches, you may—in addition to butter—use the nut spreads. Hazelnut butter, almond butter, peanut butter, cashew butter, sesame butter, and sunflower seed butter may be purchased in health food stores, but can also be made in your own kitchen.

Halvah is a sweet product, made of sesame seeds and honey. Halvah may also be used for buttering bread.

Tahini is a paste of roasted, crushed sesame seeds. It can be used for buttering bread or added to various dishes and salad dressings. Tahini may be purchased salted or unsalted or it can be made at home.

Pasta is made from flour and water. Sometimes such ingredients as eggs, spinach, or soy flour are added. Whole grain and soy pastas are more nutritional and tasty than is the common white flour pasta.

Soy noodles and *soy spaghetti* are cooked for 10 to 15 minutes.

Whole grain noodles, spaghetti, and *macaroni* are cooked for 12 minutes.

Unsalted buckwheat spaghetti, noodles, macaroni, and *vermicelli* are cooked for about 5 minutes. *Vermicelli* and *whole grain elbow macaroni* may be cooked in soup for the last 5 to 10 minutes.

Lasagne may be either yellow (with eggs) or green (with spinach). The wrapper will specify whether it has to be cooked first.

Cannelloni is pasta tubes which are filled and baked. Usually they do not need to be cooked first.

Fettucine is wide bands of spaghetti, to which has been added either egg or spinach. It is cooked for 12 minutes.

Chinese rice noodles are made from rice flour and are used very often in oriental dishes. They may also be broken in little pieces and put into soups, or they may be served as a side dish. Rice noodles are cooked for about 5 minutes.

Peas, dried. See legumes.

Rice. See grain products.

Salt. Most households use much too much salt. Salt binds fluid in the body, and this should be avoided if one suffers from certain ailments, such as high blood pressure and certain liver, kidney, and heart diseases.

If you think that life is too difficult without salt in the food, you should use sea salt. The common white table salt is a refined product, from which all minerals have been eliminated. Pure sea salt contains a number of minerals and trace minerals. See also gomasio.

When salt is mentioned in the recipes, it means the unrefined, dark sea salt. It is also a good idea to add herbs, onion, or garlic to the food. These are healthy additives, which will compensate for any lack of salty taste.

Seaweed and Algae are imported from Asia and are first and foremost used in macrobiotic cooking. (Macrobiotic living is based on the oriental principle of the two opposite life forces, yin and yang. Whole grains and beans, complemented with vegetables, play a major role in the nutritional aspect of macrobiotic life.) The vegetables from the sea are so nutritious that they ought to be utilized to a much greater extent than they now are.

Seaweed is rich in proteins, vitamins, and minerals, mainly calcium and iron, as well as trace minerals.

Seaweed has to be cleaned thoroughly before it is used. It has to be soaked in ample water ½-hour before cooking—longer if possible.

Seaweed can be used in soups, or it can be mixed with rice or grains or mixed in stews, or used as a side dish.

Wakame has a mild taste, and it is a good seaweed for the beginner. It should be cooked for about 30 minutes in a soup, or cut up very fine and cooked with rice or corn.

Kombu is used in the same way as wakame, but more sparingly, since it is rather salty.

Arame, or *iziki* and *hijiki,* is a thin, spaghetti-like, and strong-tasting seaweed. It is used as a side dish and is boiled in ample water for 30 to 40 minutes. May also be used in soups, salads, or mixed dishes such as stews.

Nori is pressed seaweed. It is heated over a flame for a short time, then crumbled over soups or other dishes.

Agar-agar is an algae product, rich in minerals. It is used as a substitute for gelatin. Use about 2½ teaspoons

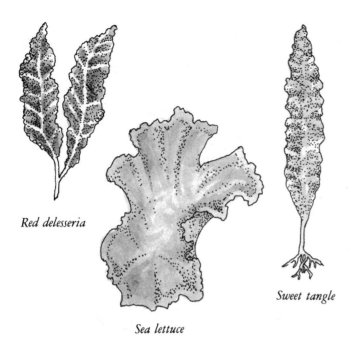

Red delesseria

Sea lettuce

Sweet tangle

Sweet Tangle is one of the most usable seaweeds. It is about a yard long. The innermost 10 inches is cut off and rinsed thoroughly. The mucilage, which consists of sugar, is washed off.

The sweet tangle is cut in rectangular pieces, which then are made into rolls. You can fill them as you do spring rolls (see page 112) or as stuffed grape leaves (see page 125). The edges of the weed are bent and the rolls then folded. The rolls may be held together with toothpicks. The seaweed rolls are fried in oil in a frying pan. During frying they will change color, turning green when they are tender and crisp, and then brown, after another 5 minutes, when done.

This seaweed can be used in the same way as all of the imported seaweeds. Another very usable seaweed is *sea lettuce*. It is a weed with very thin leaves, which often grows very close to shore. Others are *red seaweed* and *red delesseria*.

If you have the opportunity to collect large amounts of seaweed, you can dry it in a light and airy place and save it for the winter.

Seitan is made from wheat gluten. Its consistency is somewhat similar to that of meat. Seitan is a valuable protein source, which has been used in the East for several hundred years.

Seitan may be purchased by the glass, but it is very easy to make it yourself. (See page 25.) Seitan may be cut in cubes or slices and used in many different dishes. It may also be shaped and fried as hamburgers.

Soy Flour and Flakes. See grain products.

of agar-agar to 1 pint of liquid. Agar-agar is sold granulated and as flakes. The flakes are easier to work with.

There is no reason to buy expensive imported seaweeds if one lives near the coast, and if the sea is relatively clean and unpolluted. The seaweed is gathered in the summertime and can be found on the beach, washed on shore after a storm. You can also wade into the water a short way and pick it up. The seaweed is attached to stones, fishing stakes, or piers and the like. The whole plant is removed, as it is the innermost part, that which attaches to the stones, which is the youngest part of the plant, and that is the portion used for cooking.

Sweeteners are used sparingly in the vegetarian kitchen. These products are rich in carbohydrates and yield only empty calories.

Refined white sugar contains 99.8 percent carbohydrates, and it breaks down much too quickly in the body. *Unrefined sugar* is not much better, but it does contain certain minerals. *Honey* is also used sparingly. The least refined honey is the most nutritious; it contains, for instance, vitamin B2, calcium, iron, phosphorus, sodium, and potassium.

Dark cane syrup has been extracted from the sugar cane. It contains B vitamins, calcium, iron, and potassium.

Maple syrup comes, as the name implies, from the maple tree. It is a syrup with excellent taste and aroma.

Fructose also consists of easily broken down carbohydrates and should be avoided. Its sweetening capacity is half that of refined sugar.

Malt extract is similar to syrup. It is made from sprouted barley, which has been roasted, crushed, and cooked.

Tamari (Shoyu) is a soy sauce made from lactic (acid) fermented soybeans and whole wheat. Tamari is a purely natural product without any additives, and it is used as a substitute for Chinese soya to give taste in many dishes and dressings. Tamari is rich in proteins and minerals.

Tofu, a soybean curd, may be obtained either dried or packaged. Dried tofu is softened by soaking before use.

Tofu can be used in almost all dishes, in salads, soups, or on sandwiches. You can make your own tofu from crushed soybeans.

Vegetable Bouillon may come as powder, paste, or in cubes, and with or without salt.

Yeast Extract is a tasteful addition, rich in proteins, vitamins, and minerals.

HERBS & FLAVORINGS

Fresh herbs are important and healthful flavorings for vegetarian food. Herbs are rich in vitamins A, B, and C and minerals such as iron, calcium, and trace minerals.

The use of herbs goes back to the earliest civilizations. For thousands of years they have been used in cooking as well as in folk medicine, and many herbs are still being used in the modern medical industry.

The countries surrounding the Mediterranean have a long tradition of using herbs in their cooking. In Denmark, the most popular herbs have been thyme, parsley, and dill. Only during recent years have we seen a growing interest in other herbs. Herbs blend very well with vegetable dishes, and they will often be the touch that gives a dish its distinction.

It is very easy to grow your own herbs. They will grow in pots in your window or on the balcony, or they may be grown in your garden. This makes it possible to have fresh herbs all year round. Grown in the garden, the herbs will be so plentiful that you will have more than you can consume during the summer. The surplus can be frozen or dried for use in winter.

The most commonly used herbs in this book are sweet basil, watercress, savory, lemon balm, dill, tarragon, fennel, lovage, marjoram, oregano, parsley, chives, rosemary, sage, and thyme.

The French "bouquet garni," which is added as a flavoring in several dishes, consists of a small bunch of thyme and parsley plus a bay leaf. To make this, place 2 or 3 sprigs of fresh thyme, fresh parsley, and a bay leaf between two 4-inch celery stalks and tie together with white cotton string.

Dried herbs have a much stronger taste than fresh ones, and 1 to 2 teaspoonfuls of dried herbs correspond to 1 tablespoon of fresh herbs. Be guided by your taste.

Spices

Spices are dried parts of different tropical plants—the roots, the leaves, the flowers, or the seeds. Spices such as curry and caraway are often sautéed in oil before the other ingredients are added, to release their aromatic taste.

Danish taste buds are not used to the hot spices from the East; they may irritate the intestinal walls, and are therefore used in very moderate amounts.

The most commonly used spices are anise, cayenne pepper, chili powder, turmeric, ginger, cinnamon, cardamom, curry, caraway, coriander, nutmeg, cloves, paprika, and pepper.

Onions and Garlic

Onions and Garlic are used extensively in the vegetarian kitchen. Garlic is especially valued because of its many excellent qualities, and has been used in folk medicine as far back as in ancient Egypt. Garlic, considered a killer of bacteria, relieves fever and mucosity, and it regulates the blood pressure—and then, of course, it adds its own very characteristic taste to any dish.

Garlic has both avid backers and strong adversaries. Some people stay away from garlic because of its smell, but according to the culinary author Elizabeth David, the smell is supposed to decrease the more garlic one eats.

The nuisance of the smell may also be lessened if the clove of garlic is cut lengthwise and the green sprout is

removed. Furthermore, it helps to eat something green, like parsley, after garlic has been consumed.

The recipes in this book use garlic very often. It may, of course, be omitted, or you can rub the side of the bowl or casserole with a clove of cut garlic, to get only a hint of this herb.

Nature's Plants

The sprinkle of green on food usually comes from cultivated herbs and plants, but there is no reason to limit yourself to these.

During the springtime a number of wild plants may very well be used in your cooking. The wild plants are called nature's own medicine and, like herbs, have been used as medicine for thousands of years. They are rich in vitamins, minerals, and trace minerals.

The plants or their leaves are picked as young and fresh as possible, but never in areas close to heavily traveled roads.

The plants may be added to sandwiches or salads, cooked in soups, or used for stuffings.

The plants that are most easily obtained are small nettle, wild watercress, coltsfoot, chickweed, dandelion, ribgrass or plantain, and dock.

SPROUTS

Sprouts from beans, grains, and seeds add many minerals and vitamins to the food, and they should be eaten every day, especially during the winter.

It is both inexpensive and easy to grow your own sprouts. It requires neither a garden nor room on your window sill. The whole process takes place in a glass jar.

For sprouting, you should use beans, grains, or seeds that are guaranteed organically grown and that have not been treated with an insecticide or fungicide. Buy them in a health food store so that you can be sure of the quality.

For sprouting, try a ¼-cup or less of any of the following:

Alfalfa seeds	Sunflower seeds	Fenugreek seeds
Mung beans	Soybeans	Rye, barley, oat,
Lentils	Azuki beans	millet, corn, wheat

There are several sprouting methods. The glass jar method is the least complicated; you can also get plastic containers in health food stores, but they do not have any particular advantage over the quart glass jar.

How to Sprout

First, check over the seeds or beans, and discard any that are cracked. Rinse the seeds in a sieve, then soak them in the glass jar, using 4 times as much water as seeds. Small seeds should be soaked for about 8 hours, larger seeds and beans for about 15 hours.

After soaking, rinse the seeds, leaving only the water that naturally clings to the seeds. Place the top on the jar. Use the metal lid, with holes punched in it, for the beans and larger seeds, and cheesecloth held in place by a rubber band for the smaller seeds.

Establish a routine of rinsing and draining the seeds 3 times a day. Keep the jar on its side. There is disagreement over whether the sprouting seeds should be kept in the dark. I advise some darkened place, such as a kitchen closet. Bring the seeds into the light 1 day before you use them. By doing this, chlorophyll will be created, and the sprouts will turn light green.

Continue to rinse the seeds until the sprouts have grown the desired length. Most seeds take from 3 to 5 days, but mung beans and soybeans may take 6 to 8 days. As the sprouts grow, they will gain about 8 times their weight, which means that 2 ounces of seeds will yield a pound of sprouts.

Sprouts are eaten with the seed's shell, from which they have grown. True, the sprout has used up the nourishment, but the shells provide an excellent fiber food.

The sprouts may be kept in the refrigerator for, at most, a week.

Sprouts may be eaten as they are, or they may be sprinkled on different dishes such as salads, soups, stews, and sandwiches. They should not be cooked, since this causes a loss of minerals and vitamins.

All over the world research has been done on the nutritional value of sprouts. Many, not always concurring, results have been reached, but all agree that sprouts are important as a food supplement. American researchers estimate an increase of 10 to 1,350 percent of the B vitamin group contained in sprouted oats. In sprouted wheat, the increase of vitamin C is said to be in the neighborhood of 600 percent. The vitamin E and K contents are also believed to be increased considerably.

LACTIC ACID FERMENTATION

Acetic acid fermentation is nature's own preservation method, and it is, with drying, one of the world's oldest. The method has all but disappeared in the western world, where it is now used principally when making sauerkraut, which is fermented cabbage, and sour milk products.

In the East, Russia, and the Balkans, the tradition is still kept alive. For example, the Russian borsch is traditionally made with beets fermented with lactic acid. In the East, miso is an indispensable part of the daily diet. The fermentation of miso is a process that takes years during which the highly indigestible soy protein is refined and becomes a product that is easy to digest. The true Chinese soy sauce, too, is a lactic acid-fermented product.

For lactic acid fermentation, the vegetables are finely cut. During the fermentation process, the lactose of the vegetables is converted into lactic acid. The acidifying of products not only means that they will keep longer, but it will also refine and improve their taste.

Lactic acid-fermented vegetables are easily digested and have a balancing effect on the gastric juices. The lactic acid bacteria prevent putrefaction, not only in the vegetables, but also in the intestines. The blood circulation in the intestines is increased and the digestion eased when these vegetables are eaten.

Acidified vegetables are firm but tender, and they have a very piquant aroma. They may be used as they are, for example in salads, or they may be added to various hot dishes, but preferably as late in the cooking process as possible, so they will be warmed but not lose their enzymes.

In lactic acid fermentation, use vegetables whose growth has not been forced through heavy feeding of fertilizers, and they must under no circumstances have been sprayed with pesticides. If they have been sprayed, the fermentation will not be successful, and the vegetables will rot.

To start the fermentation, a specific salt concentration, pressure on the vegetables, and a specific temperature are required.

In Denmark, special glass jars for lactic acid fermentation are sold. These come in two sizes, holding about ten and fifteen quarts. However, you can make do with ordinary canning jars. In North America, large glass jars or stoneware crocks are often used, and if the sauerkraut is to be stored for some time, it is transferred to canning jars. The most important things, in any event, are that air be kept from the vegetables during the process, and that the vegetables be kept under pressure.

The pressure is created by placing a small plate upside down over the vegetables, then placing a heavy article, a stone for example, on top of the plate. The stone must be boiled first; all other articles used for the lactic acid fermentation must be absolutely clean. Glass must be scalded and air-dried. Never use detergents.

Sauerkraut

Those trying fermentation for the first time are urged to try cabbage and make sauerkraut.

Make sure all containers and utensils are clean.

Remove the outermost leaves of the cabbage, then quarter it and remove the core. Chop it into shreds the thickness of a dime.

You may, at this time, add small amounts of other ingredients, such as caraway seeds, juniper berries, coriander, or chopped apples, for different flavors.

Weigh the cabbage and measure the sea salt to be used on the basis of 1.5 percent as much salt as cabbage. This figures out to 3½ tablespoons of salt for 10 pounds of cabbage.

Press the cabbage down in the jar until the juice appears. Place a whole, clean cabbage leaf on top.

Make a brine of the salt and enough water to cover the cabbage by boiling the salt and water, then letting it cool. Pour it over the cabbage until the brine is about 1 inch above the cabbage. There should be airspace enough, too, for the next step, placing the plate and stone on top of the cabbage. The glass container is now closed.

It should stand for 2 to 3 days in temperatures of 70 to 75 °F, then be moved to a cooler area, 59 to 60 °F is ideal,

for 3 to 4 weeks. The sauerkraut is then ready for use, and should be put in the refrigerator.

Editor's note: This method varies from American methods in which a large, open crock is used for making the sauerkraut, a stronger brine is made, and the sauerkraut is canned; this can be used by those who do not have the special jars for the process.

In *Keeping the Harvest* (Garden Way Publishing), authors Nancy Chioffi and Gretchen Mead suggest these steps for krauting:

1. Use heavy, firm heads of cabbage. Trim off outer leaves and wash the heads. Cut heads into quarters, remove core, and slice into thin shreds.

2. Weigh cabbage, then mix in "pickling" or "canning" salt at the rate of 3 tablespoons per 5 pounds of cabbage.

3. Let it settle for 20 or 30 minutes, then pack the cabbage firmly into a clean crock, pressing with hands or a wooden spoon to remove air pockets and to draw the juice. Leave at least 6 inches of space at the top of the crock.

4. Place a heavy-duty plastic bag on the cabbage, fill it with water, then tie the top. This bag excludes air from the crock and presses down on the cabbage.

5. Put the container in 68 to 72 °F temperature.

6. If, in 24 hours, brine doesn't cover the cabbage, add a 2½ percent brine (1½ tablespoons of salt per quart of water).

7. Check kraut daily. If scum appears, remove it with a spoon. Add brine if needed to cover kraut.

8. Let kraut ferment for 5 to 6 weeks, until bubbles no longer appear on the surface.

9. To process for storage, heat kraut to simmering (185 to 210°F) in its own juice. Stir gently. Add 2½ percent brine if there isn't enough to cover the kraut. Pack into clean, hot canning jars, press down to release air bubbles, and cover with hot juice, leaving a ½-inch of headroom. Tighten lids and process in a boiling water bath, 15 minutes for pints, 20 minutes for quarts. Place on a rack, several inches apart, to cool.

Other Vegetables

In addition to cabbage, you can use this process with beets, cucumbers, beans, onions, radishes, carrots, celery, mushrooms, green peas, tomatoes, and turnips, and you can add such spices as bay leaves, mustard seeds, coriander, dill, tarragon, horseradish, ginger, and garlic.

Beets and other roots are chopped and treated the same way as cabbage.

Mushrooms and beans are cut into small pieces and boiled for a few minutes in the salt water, then cooled before being placed in the glass jar.

Vegetables may be treated alone, or mixed with other vegetables. Some possible combinations are celery and parsnips, carrots and onions with garlic and dill, and cucumbers and beans with onions, mustard, and dill.

You won't be left in doubt if something goes wrong. Both taste and smell will tell you. The most common reason is that the vegetables used were of inferior quality. It also may be that the yeast fungus took over and spoiled the lactic acid bacteria because the jar or crock was placed in too warm an area.

Sometimes, too, a white yeast fungus may appear at the top of the jar. If it does, remove it with a spoon.

SEITAN

Seitan, often used as a meat substitute, is a wheat gluten product which has been eaten by Buddhist monks in the temples of the East for centuries. Seitan was brought to the West by those who practice macrobiotic cooking, and is highly valued by many vegetarians, and perhaps more so by their meat-eating guests, since its consistency is very similar to meat.

Seitan may be purchased by the jar, but it is easy to make.

4 cups whole grain flour
2 cups lukewarm water
4 tablespoons tamari
Wakame or Sweet Tangle seaweed

Measure flour into a bowl and add enough lukewarm water, while stirring, to make a stiff dough. Knead it well for several minutes. Form a dough ball and cover it with lukewarm water. Let it stand for about 30 minutes. During this time the gluten fibers contract and the starch can then be worked out of the dough.

To do this, work the dough, a little at a time, with your fingers, keeping the dough in the water. Put the worked dough in a sieve over a bowl of water. Continue until you have washed all of the dough. Rinse it all in 4 to 6 changes of water until all the starch is removed. The first and last rinsing water must be cold; the others can be lukewarm.

Knead the gluten dough until it becomes a firm mass. Put tamari and pre-soaked seaweed into a casserole dish with the gluten dough. Add enough water to cover and cook it for about 45 minutes.

Let it cool, then roll it out until it is about ½ inch thick. Use a glass to cut out "hamburgers" which can then be fried golden in oil. The Seitan can also be cut into small cubes and cooked in soups or stews.

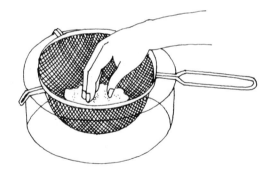

Seitan Burgers

The Seitan hamburgers may be used as meat would be. Split a roll or open a pita (Arabic pocket bread) and spread with tahini, sandwich spread, or natural mustard. Put in a leaf of lettuce, then the cooked Seitan hamburger, and sprinkle with tamari. Sauerkraut, sprouts, or watercress may be added to this burger.

This recipe will yield about 8 Seitan burgers, but you can make a larger amount of Seitan, since it will keep for some time in the refrigerator.

Seitan Seaweed Rolls

When cooking Seitan, you can add enough seaweed to make seaweed rolls. Cut the cooked Seitan in rectangular pieces, then roll in the seaweed and add finely chopped olives or onions. The seaweed rolls can be put in an ovenproof dish and warmed in the oven.

Many vegetarians use the gluten (without the tamari and seaweed) as the basic ingredient of recipes that call for the addition of meat-like seasoning, peppers, onions, and oil, then suggest either frying individual servings or baking as a loaf.

UTENSILS

The preparation of vegetarian food does not require utensils other than those used in most households. If, however, you eat a lot of raw vegetable salads or finely cut vegetables, it would probably pay to acquire a good electric food processor. This comes with various sized accessories for grating and shredding, and some models feature an attachment that will process beans, grains, sesame seeds, and nuts.

If you don't want to invest in an electric food processor, you can very well make do with a manually operated machine, many different models of which are available, or you can use an ordinary grater.

A masher is very good for puréeing potatoes and vegetables. A good brush will often do most of the necessary cleaning of vegetables. They may be scraped afterwards with a knife. A good selection of glass bowls for food preparation is preferred to the brightly colored plastic bowls.

Ovenproof bowls and dishes are very often used in veg-

etarian cooking. Choose utensils of ovenproof glass or with a white, lead-free glaze. Use pots and pans of stainless steel and iron.

For steaming vegetables, use a colander. Put the vegetables in it, then place the colander into a pot. The water in the pot should not reach the vegetables. Use a top on the pot. This way the vegetables will lose less of their nutritional value.

HANDLING VEGETABLES

Vegetables should be kept in a dark, cool place, and used as quickly as possible. During wintertime it may be difficult, if not impossible, to get certain fresh vegetables. If you can't, select the frozen rather than canned vegetables.

Wash vegetables just before cooking. Where possible, the peel of both vegetables and fruits should be eaten, since much of the nourishment comes from it. Furthermore, the peels, skins, and rinds make excellent fiber supplements.

Vegetables should be cooked for as short a time as possible since beneficial nutrients are lost when they are subjected to heat.

Save the water in which vegetables are cooked and use it in soups and sauces. Never cook more than what will be eaten at once (unless you need some for next day's sandwiches) since nutrients will be lost.

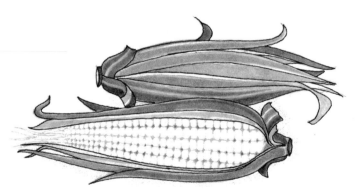

Combination of Courses

An everyday meal most often consists of a single course with salad, and perhaps with bread and potatoes prepared in one way or another. If time permits, you may make a traditional dinner with hors d'oeuvres or soup and a main course with side dishes. But with vegetarian cooking an exciting possibility is to serve several small vegetable courses at the same time. As much as possible, try to avoid offering the same vegetable in more than one dish, and eggs or milk products in more than one dish. Choose the vegetables of the season and those native to your region.

Food prepared with joy, love, and interest is tastiest, and if there is harmony in its color combination, one is sure to have created an esthetic meal.

The recipes that follow are calculated to serve 4 persons, unless otherwise mentioned, but it will be necessary to experiment with the size of the portions. Some eat more than others. Whether the portions will be sufficient will also depend on how many courses are being served.

If you want to avoid milk, you may substitute vegetable bouillon in most of the recipes. Where no fat percentage is given for cream, either half and half or whipping cream may be used.

BREAKFAST

It is important to start the day right, and breakfast is important for your well being during the entire day.

When your body gets a solid, healthful breakfast, you will not be so tempted by little in-between-meal snacks.

A dish of porridge or soaked muesli is very good for starting your day. Both may be eaten with milk products, fresh fruit, homemade fruit purées, sauces and, finely cut nuts. Milk products with muesli and fruit sauces or mashed fruits—or whole grain bread with cheese—present other possibilities. Fresh fruit and/or raw vegetables should always be on your breakfast table.

OATMEAL

1½ cups steel-cut oats*
4 cups water
Salt, if desired

Soak oats in the water overnight. Bring to a boil, and boil for about 40 to 60 minutes, or until the oats are translucent and tender. Add more water, if necessary. A pinch of salt may be added when oats are cooked.

*Rolled oats (quick-cooking or old-fashioned) do not require overnight soaking. See package for cooking directions.

DRY MUESLI

1 cup wheat germ
1 cup roasted oats
½ cup sesame seeds
¼ cup sunflower seeds
¼ cup almond or nut flakes

Mix ingredients and keep in a glass, tightly closed jar until used.

Dry muesli may be sprinkled on yogurt, or eaten with sliced fresh or dried fruits.

BIRCHER-BENNER MUESLI

4 tablespoons oats
¾ cup cold water
4 tablespoons lemon juice
4 tablespoons yogurt
Honey or fresh fruit juice
4 big apples
4 tablespoons sliced almonds or other nuts

Soak the oats in water overnight. In the morning, mix lemon juice and yogurt with the soaked oats. If necessary, a little more water may be added.

Honey or fruit juice and grated apples are stirred into the muesli. Sprinkle with almonds or nuts. The muesli is served at once.

Crushed wheat, rye, barley, wheat germ, millet flakes, etc. may be mixed in the muesli, and you may use other fruits than apples.

MILLET PORRIDGE

4 cups water
1 cup whole millet
Salt, if desired

Bring water to a boil and stir in millet. Lower heat, and simmer the porridge, covered, for 20 to 25 minutes, or until grain is tender and water is absorbed. A dash of salt may be added when millet is cooked.

BARLEY PORRIDGE

1 cup coarsely cracked barley
2 cups water
4 tablespoons raisins
Salt, if desired

Soak barley overnight. Bring 2 cups water to a boil, add barley, cover, and cook over low heat for about 10 minutes, or until water is absorbed. Stir occasionally. Add the raisins during the last 5 minutes. Add a dash of salt, if desired.

WHOLE GRAIN PORRIDGE

1 cup cracked wheat, rye, barley, or
    oats, or a mixture of these
2 cups water
Salt, if desired

Soak the cracked grains in water overnight. Bring water and grain to a boil,
stir, cover, lower heat and cook porridge
for 30 to 40 minutes or until water is
absorbed. A dash of salt may be added
when grain is cooked.

BUCKWHEAT PORRIDGE

4 cups water
1 cup buckwheat grits
Salt, if desired

Bring water to a boil and add the buckwheat grits. Stir. Lower heat and simmer, covered, for 10–20 minutes. Stir
occasionally, and add a bit more water, if
needed. A sprinkle of salt may be added
when grits are cooked.

MIXED PORRIDGE

¼ cup whole millet
¼ cup cracked buckwheat
¼ cup oats
4 tablespoons linseeds
4 tablespoons sunflower seeds
½ cup dried prunes, cut up
4 cups water

Soak all ingredients overnight. Bring
the water and ingredients to a boil,
lower the heat, and simmer the porridge
for about 20 minutes. Stir it now and
then. A dash of salt can be added.

All grain products should be soaked
overnight. It will shorten the cooking
time and make the porridge easier to digest.

It is difficult to say exactly how much
water is to be used when cooking porridge. Watch it during the cooking, so
that it doesn't burn, and add more water
as necessary. The goal is to use just
enough water so that the porridge is
cooked when the water is absorbed.

Different kinds of porridge can be
made by adding linseeds, or dried,
soaked fruits, such as prunes, figs, dates,
or apricots. You can also eat the porridge with milk alone, milk and honey,
fresh fruits, dry muesli, or homemade
mashed fruit, such as this:

PRUNE AND FIG MASH

½ pound figs
½ pound prunes

Soak for 8 hours in as much water as
will cover the fruit.

Cut prunes and figs in small pieces.
Cook them in the water in which they
were soaked until most of the liquid has
evaporated— about 15 minutes. Stir occasionally.

If you have digestion problems, you
may cook 6–8 senna leaves in the mash.
However, senna should not be eaten reg-
ularly, as it may cause a diarrhea-like
condition; eat a maximum of 1 tablespoon daily of the mash.

One may make a larger amount than
suggested above. The mash can be refrigerated in jars with tight lids. It will
keep for a couple of weeks.

LUNCH

In a country like Denmark, where people have such deep-rooted traditions about sandwiches, lunch can create problems for a novice vegetarian. The vegetarian kitchen has nothing that resembles salami, bologna, or head-cheese. But there are lots of other possibilities. If you do not want to give up sandwiches, you can, first of all, consider a number of pâtés, rissoles, and vegetable hamburgers, which are very well suited for sandwiches. Many times the leftovers from last night's dinner may also be used, and if they are too juicy to be put on bread, they can be taken to work in a plastic container.

If it is not the end of the world if you do not have

sandwiches for lunch, you can take a raw vegetable salad. With this you may have homemade whole grain bread, leftovers from dinner the night before, or cottage cheese. A carrot or some fresh fruit can complete the lunch.

If you eat lunch at home, or if you want to spend a little more time preparing your lunch, you can make a combination of different dishes from the chapter containing side dishes and hors d'oeuvres.

Suggestions for Sandwiches

For a sandwich base use homemade, whole grain sourdough bread. See recipe page 168. The bread may be spread with butter or tahini or eaten plain. Put a leaf of lettuce on the bread, unless the sandwich has to be taken to work wrapped in paper. In this case, it will lose its freshness before lunch, and it would be better to take a mixed salad.

In addition to pâté and rissoles, the following can be used:

- A slice of cooked celery with grated carrot and lemon juice as desired.

- Cooked leeks with grated horseradish and watercress.

- Potato sticks, fried raw and dipped in fatless mayonnaise; for decoration, add red pepper and black olives.

- Scrambled eggs with tomato slices and chopped chives.

- Farmer's cheese, 5 percent fat content mixed with cucumber and finely chopped red and green peppers, with chopped herbs added to taste.

- Sliced, boiled new potatoes, garnished with sliced avocado, dipped in lemon juice and dill weed.

- Avocado slices, dipped in lemon juice and garnished with red or white Bermuda onion and alfalfa sprouts.

- Cottage cheese, garnished with sliced radishes, fresh green peas, and fresh, chopped chives.

- Cottage cheese, garnished with sliced avocado, dipped in lemon juice with either fresh, chopped chives or parsley.

- Sliced mushrooms mixed with farmer's cheese (5 percent fat content) and chopped parsley and red or white Bermuda onions added to taste, garnished with watercress.

- Fried onions with sliced tomatoes, sprinkled with grated cheese.

- Fried tofu garnished with sliced tomatoes and watercress.

- Farmer's cheese (5 percent fat content), mixed with raisins and garnished with sliced banana.

A more elaborate and festive sandwich could be made with:

- Boiled, green asparagus, sprinkled with crushed thyme. Add a slice of cheese and broil until cheese is golden.

- Mushrooms in cream sauce on toast.

- Sliced mushrooms fried with chopped onions and parsley. Put on toast, add grated Emmenthal cheese and broil until cheese is golden.

- Fried onions spread on slices of bread; add sliced hard-boiled eggs, and pour a sauce, made with sour cream, grated apples, and curry powder to taste, over the sandwich.

- Tomato, sliced and sprinkled with sweet basil, topped with green olive halves and sliced cheese. Broil until cheese is golden.

- Slices of cold herb pâté (see recipe) topped with a ring of green pepper. Fill pepper rings with mushrooms in cream sauce.

Tahini and hummus (see recipe below) are particularly used in the vegetarian kitchen. Tahini, a Mideast seed butter, may be used as a spread instead of butter, and it can be added to many dishes as a flavoring.

Hummus is made of garbanzo beans mashed into a pâté. It may be used for sandwiches or put into Arabic pocket bread (pita).

HUMMUS

1½ cups garbanzo beans
About ½ cup olive oil
Lemon juice
2 cloves garlic
Salt
1 bunch parsley, finely chopped

Soak the beans overnight and cook until tender, about 1 hour. Drain and press through a sieve, or purée in blender.

Mix or blend the paste with olive oil and lemon juice, until it attains a smooth consistency. Add pressed garlic and salt. You may also add tahini.

Remove from blender and add parsley. The paste must be rather stiff. If it becomes too firm, it may be thinned with a little water.

TAHINI

1½ cups sesame seeds
Water
Salt

Toast sesame seeds lightly in a dry frying pan, then pound in a mortar or use a blender. When a paste is formed, mix with boiled, lukewarm water until smooth. Salt may be added to taste.

SANDWICH PASTE

½ pound black olives
2 ounces capers
1 clove garlic
4 tablespoons olive oil

Pit the olives. Pound the meat of the olives in a mortar together with the drained capers, pressed garlic, and oil. You may also use a blender for this process.

The sandwich paste keeps well in the refrigerator. It is used as a sandwich spread or a filling (for pita) together with sliced tomatoes, lettuce, and bean sprouts, or with cheese.

SALADS

Raw vegetables play a central role in the vegetarian menu. They have not lost vitamins, minerals, and trace minerals through cooking, so they should make up the greater part of the vegetarian's daily food intake.

Different health conscious movements recommend starting any hot meal with a fresh vegetable salad. The well-known Swiss nutrition researcher, Dr. Bircher-Benner, is one of the advocates of this idea. He even recommends that one-half of the daily meals should consist of raw vegetables. He attributes great importance to raw vegetables because of their favorable effect on the intestinal flora, and he believes that the fatigue that may occur

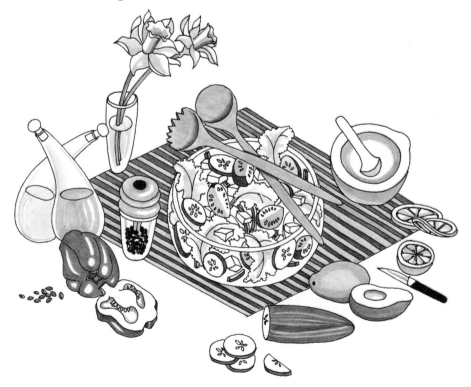

after having consumed a hot meal can be avoided if the meal is started with a raw vegetable salad.

As far as I know, this belief has not been scientifically proven, but it is certain that starting a meal with a raw vegetable salad has several advantages, not least of which is that they have a filling effect, thus lessening the temptation to eat too much of more fattening foods.

Preparation

Vegetables should be cleaned by thorough rinsing, but they should not be left in water for any length of time. They can be grated, sliced, or cut in small pieces. Many of their green tops can be used for sprinkling over salads.

Fresh vegetable salads should be prepared immediately prior to serving, as exposure to oxygen decreases their nutritional value, especially the vitamin C content. Red cabbage may be cut 15 minutes before it is to be used. It should be put in a dressing of equal parts of honey and vinegar or lemon juice and allowed to soak. The acidification improves the taste and looks of the cabbage.

Wild Plants

Wild plants can be used extensively in salads during spring and summer months. As already mentioned, wild plants must be collected from areas away from motor traffic, and where you can be sure no poisonous spraying has taken place.

Wild plants contain vital nutritional substances not found in cultured plants, and for this reason they benefit the diet.

Since not everyone can collect wild plants, they have been mentioned in only a few recipes, but they can be used in all salads when available.

CHEESE-AVOCADO SALAD

2 avocados
½ pound cheddar cheese
¼ pound blue grapes
¼ cup walnuts, chopped
4 tablespoons oil
2 tablespoons herbal vinegar
Alfalfa sprouts

Peel and dice avocados. Dice the cheese. Cut grapes in half and remove seeds. Mix these 3 ingredients with chopped walnuts and stir in the oil and vinegar dressing. Sprinkle with alfalfa sprouts.

RED AVOCADO SALAD

2 avocados
1 cup pickled or fresh grated beets
1 salad onion (red or white Bermuda)
3 tablespoons oil
3 tablespoons lemon juice
Wheat sprouts

Peel and dice avocados. Mix with beets and chopped onion. Blend oil and lemon juice and pour over the salad. Mix. Sprinkle with lots of wheat or other sprouts.

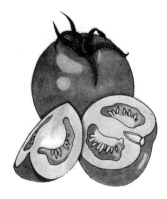

AVOCADO SALAD

2 avocados
1 shallot
2 tomatoes
¼ pound mushrooms
¼ cucumber
4 tablespoons corn oil
2 tablespoons herbal vinegar
1 bunch of chives

Peel and dice avocados. Chop shallot and cut tomatoes in quarters. Slice mushrooms and cucumber. Mix all of these ingredients in a salad dressing of oil and vinegar. Chop chives and sprinkle on top.

PINEAPPLE-ONION SALAD

1 small pineapple
1 big onion
1 cup crème fraîche* or sour cream (18 percent fat content)
Curry
Paprika
Tamari
2 tablespoons finely chopped lemon balm

Peel the pineapple and cut it into small cubes. Chop onion and pour boiling water over it. Let stand 2 minutes, drain, and mix with the pineapple.

Add curry, paprika, and tamari to the sour cream according to taste. Fold pineapple and onion into the sour cream. Sprinkle lemon balm on top.

*To make crème fraîche, mix 1 tablespoon sour cream with 1 cup heavy cream, and leave it at room temperature for 8 hours. Refrigerate it until ready for use. It will keep for 4–5 days.

BANANA SALAD

1–2 bananas
4 tablespoons honegar (equal parts
  honey and cider vinegar)
2 tablespoons olive oil
¼ cup raisins
½ cup shredded coconut
1 large Belgian endive

Slice the bananas and mix at once with
honegar and oil. Add raisins and shredded coconut. Cut up endive and mix.
  This salad is delicious with oriental
food.

MIXED CAULIFLOWER SALAD

2 cups cauliflowerettes
1 cup finely chopped red cabbage
½ cup peas, shelled
1 handful alfalfa sprouts
¼ cup chopped pumpkin seeds
4 tablespoons olive oil
2 tablespoons lemon juice

Mix cauliflower and red cabbage. Add
peas, sprouts, and seeds. Mix oil and
lemon juice and pour over salad.

CAULIFLOWER SALAD WITH BLUE CHEESE DRESSING

2 cups cauliflowerettes
½ cup iceberg lettuce, shredded
1 cucumber, sliced
2 ounces blue cheese
¾ cup yogurt
2 tablespoons olive oil
2 tomatoes
Watercress

Mix cauliflower and shredded lettuce.
Add sliced cucumber. Mix cheese in to
the yogurt with the oil. Pour this dressing over the vegetables and garnish with
tomato wedges and watercress.

BEAN SALAD

½ cup dried lima beans
6 tablespoons olive oil
3 tablespoons herbal vinegar
1 clove garlic
1½ teaspoons total of crushed oregano,
  basil, rosemary
1 shallot
½ cucumber
2–3 tomatoes
1 bunch of parsley

Wash beans and soak them overnight.
Cook until tender in the same water,
about 1 hour. Drain, and when cool,
pour the dressing over beans. The dressing is made of the oil and vinegar,
mixed with pressed garlic and herbs.
The beans should soak in the dressing
for about 2 hours.
  Chop the shallot finely. Dice the cucumber and cut the tomatoes in wedges.
Just before the salad is served, mix vegetables and beans together. A dash of salt
and pepper may be added to taste. Sprinkle with chopped parsley.

SALAD NICOISE

½ cup dried lima beans
¼ cucumber
3–4 tomatoes
1 small onion
1 green pepper
1 bunch of radishes
2 tablespoons capers
12 black olives
1 tablespoon fresh, chopped basil
1 tablespoon olive oil
2 tablespoons herbal vinegar

Wash the beans and soak overnight. Cook until tender in the same water, about 1 hour. Drain and let cool.

Dice the cucumber, slice the tomatoes, chop the onion finely, cut the pepper into thin strips, and slice the radishes.

Mix the vegetables with the beans, and add the capers, olives, and chopped basil.

Mix a dressing of oil and vinegar and pour over the salad. A pinch of salt and pepper may be added to taste.

There are numerous variations of Salad Nicoise. Often boiled potatoes are used.

GARBANZO SALAD

1 cup garbanzo beans
4 tablespoons olive oil
3 tablespoons wine vinegar
4 iceberg lettuce leaves
2 tomatoes
1 bunch parsley

Rinse the garbanzo beans and soak overnight. Cook until tender in the same water, about 60 minutes. Drain and toss in the oil and vinegar dressing. Chill a couple of hours before serving.

At the time of serving, mix the shredded lettuce leaves with the beans, and garnish the salad with tomato wedges and parsley.

RED AND GREEN BEAN SALAD

½ cup azuki beans
1 cup fresh green beans
1 Belgian endive or chicory
¼ iceberg lettuce
1 small shallot
2 tablespoons freshly chopped savory
5 tablespoons olive oil
2 tablespoons herbal vinegar

Wash the azuki beans and soak them overnight. Cook until tender in the same water, about 1 hour. Drain and let them cool.

Cook the green beans for about 5 minutes and plunge in ice water. Then cut in small pieces.

Tear, or shred, the 2 kinds of salad greens into small pieces and chop the onions finely.

Mix the first 5 ingredients with chopped savory and serve with an oil and vinegar dressing.

BEAN SPROUT SALAD

1 cup bean sprouts
2 tangerines
2 apples
¼ cup raisins
5 tablespoons oil
2 tablespoons lemon juice
Honey

Chop the bean sprouts. Peel the tangerines and separate into sections. Dice the apples and mix those 3 ingredients with the raisins. Mix oil and lemon juice and add honey to taste. Pour the dressing over and toss the salad.

INDIAN SALAD

½ pound green beans
1 cup mushrooms, sliced
1 salad onion
½ cup crème fraîche or sour cream
Curry
2 tomatoes
1 bunch chives

Boil beans for 2–3 minutes, then drain and cut in half. Slice mushrooms and onions very thin.

Add curry and salt to the sour cream according to taste and pour over the vegetables. Garnish with tomato wedges and chopped chives.

HARICOTS VERTS SALAD

1 pound fresh green beans
1 salad onion (red or white Bermuda)
1 green pepper
2 tomatoes
5 tablespoons olive oil
3 tablespoons tarragon vinegar
1 teaspoon crushed thyme

Boil the beans for about 5 minutes. Let cool, then mix with sliced salad onion, chopped green pepper, and tomato wedges. Mix oil and vinegar with the crushed thyme and pour over the salad.

MUSHROOMS WITH CHIVES

¾ pound mushrooms
½ cup sour cream (18% fat content)
   or crème fraîche
Lemon juice
1 bunch chives
10 stuffed olives

Slice the mushrooms. Add lemon juice, with a dash of salt if desired, to the sour cream or crème fraîche, according to taste. Add chopped chives. Pour dressing over the mushrooms and garnish with sliced stuffed olives.

MUSHROOM SALAD

½ pound mushrooms
1 bunch radishes
1 green pepper
1 cup shelled peas
5 tablespoons oil
3 tablespoons lemon juice
Shredded (stinging) nettle leaves
   or watercress

Slice mushrooms and radishes. Dice the pepper. Mix all with the peas and pour oil and lemon juice dressing over the salad. Sprinkle with chopped greens.

CARROT SALAD

4 carrots
¼ cup orange juice
2 tablespoons nuts
1 cup cottage cheese
Watercress

Grate the carrots and put into the orange juice; add chopped nuts.

Put the cottage cheese in the center of a dish and arrange the grated carrots in a ring around it. Garnish with watercress.

SWEET CARROT SALAD

4 carrots
2–3 apples
Juice from ½ lemon
2 teaspoons honey
½ cup figs
4 tablespoons walnuts, chopped

Grate carrots and apples. Mix lemon juice and honey and pour over salad.

Cut figs—which you may have soaked in water for a couple of hours—in small pieces and add to the salad. Sprinkle with chopped walnuts.

GRAPEFRUIT SALAD

1 grapefruit
2 stalks of celery
1–2 Belgian endives
1 cup bean sprouts
½ cup yogurt
Honey
8 black olives
Watercress

Peel the grapefruit and split into sections. Remove the membrane and cut grapefruit into small pieces.

Cut celery and endives finely. Cut bean sprouts in half and mix first 5 ingredients. Add honey to the yogurt to taste, pour over salad and toss. At serving time garnish salad with olives and watercress.

KALE SALAD

2½ cups finely chopped kale
1½ cups finely chopped cabbage
2 carrots
10–15 dates
¾ cup yogurt
Honey

Mix kale and cabbage. Grate carrots and dice dates. Mix carrots and dates with kale and cabbage. Add honey to the yogurt to taste, pour over the salad, and toss.

SPRING SALAD

A couple of handfuls of young dandelion leaves
A couple of handfuls of nettle leaves
1 head of lettuce
1 tablespoon chopped shallot
1 tablespoon chopped chervil
5 tablespoons oil
2 tablespoons herbal vinegar
1 clove garlic

Cut dandelion, nettle, and lettuce in small pieces and mix with shallot and chervil. Pour a dressing of oil, vinegar, and pressed garlic over the salad.

COLE SLAW

1 carrot
1 green pepper
1 sweet apple
3 cups finely shredded cabbage
4 tablespoons grated cheddar cheese
4 tablespoons sunflower seeds
4 tablespoons sunflower oil
2 tablespoons grated vinegar

Grate the carrot, dice green peppper and apple. Mix ingredients with shredded cabbage. Sprinkle cheese on the salad together with chopped sunflower seeds.

Mix oil and vinegar and pour over salad.

CABBAGE SALAD

3 cups finely shredded cabbage
2 sweet apples
2 tablespoons raisins
2 tablespoons almonds, flaked
4 tablespoons corn oil
2 tablespoons honegar (half honey, half cider vinegar)

Mix the shredded cabbage with diced apples, raisins, and almond flakes. Mix oil and honegar and pour over salad.

WALNUT CABBAGE

1 green pepper
1 cup grapes
3 cups finely chopped cabbage
2 tablespoons raisins
4 tablespoons chopped walnuts
4 tablespoons walnut oil
2 tablespoons herbal vinegar

Cut pepper into thin strips. Cut grapes in half and remove seeds.

Mix cabbage, pepper, grapes, raisins, and chopped walnuts. Pour oil and vinegar dressing over the salad.

ICEBERG LETTUCE SALAD

1 small head of iceberg lettuce
½ cucumber
1 small green pepper
10 green olives
4 tablespoons olive oil
2 tablespoons lemon juice
1 teaspoon thyme
Watercress

Cut lettuce in small pieces. Dice cucumber and pepper. Slice green olives.

Mix and shake a dressing of oil, lemon juice, and crushed thyme. Pour dressing over salad and toss well. Garnish generously with watercress.

JERUSALEM ARTICHOKE SALAD

¾ pound Jerusalem artichokes
4 tablespoons olive oil
2 tablespoons herbal vinegar
4 slices pineapple
1 green pepper
2 tablespoons chopped nuts
Watercress

Use only the thickest part of the Jerusalem artichoke, as the thin parts are difficult to chew. Cut the artichoke into paper thin slices and toss immediately in the oil and vinegar dressing.

Dice the pineapple slices and chop the green pepper finely. Add to Jerusalem artichokes, and garnish with chopped nuts and watercress.

GREEN BELGIAN ENDIVE SALAD

2 Belgian endives
1 green pepper
1 stalk celery
1 cucumber
½ cup peas, shelled
4 tablespoons olive oil
2 tablespoons sesame seeds
2 tablespoons herbal vinegar
1 handful alfalfa sprouts

Chop endives and green pepper finely. Slice celery and cucumber finely. Shell peas.

Mix vegetables and pour an oil and vinegar dressing over them. Sprinkle with sesame seeds and sprouts.

BELGIAN ENDIVE SALAD

2–3 Belgian endives
1 cup bean sprouts
4 tablespoons oil
2 tablespoons herbal vinegar
4 slices whole grain white bread
3 tablespoons oil
1 clove garlic
4 tablespoons dill weed

Combine shredded endives and cut bean sprouts. Mix. Pour an oil and vinegar dressing over them.

Cut the bread into small cubes and fry until golden in oil with pressed garlic. Sprinkle bread cubes over the salad with freshly cut dill weed, just before serving.

POTATO SALAD WITH BEAN SPROUTS

1 pound potatoes
1 cup bean sprouts
1 bunch radishes
3 stalks celery
½ cup sour cream (18% fat content) or crème fraîche
4 tablespoons honegar (half honey, half cider vinegar)
¼ cup chopped celery leaves
1 bunch parsley

Cook potatoes, peel, and let cool. Slice the potatoes and mix with bean sprouts; add sliced radishes and celery.

Mix honegar, chopped celery leaves, and chopped parsley with the sour cream. You may add a pinch of salt or pepper to taste. Pour the dressing over the salad and toss.

MULTICOLORED POTATO SALAD

1 pound potatoes
1–2 avocados
1½ cups finely chopped red cabbage
¼ cup black olives, halved
4 tablespoons chopped walnuts
5 tablespoons walnut oil
3 tablespoons herbal vinegar
Watercress

Cook the potatoes, peel, let cool, and slice. Peel the avocados and cut into cubes. Mix potatoes, red cabbage, and avocados. Add cut black olives and walnut bits.

Mix the dressing and pour over salad. Sprinkle generously with watercress.

UNDERGROUND SALAD

¾ pound potatoes
2 beets
¼ celeriac root
6 tablespoons corn oil
3 tablespoons lemon juice
1 parsnip
1 bunch dill

Cook potatoes and beets together. Remove potatoes when they are done. Peel the celeriac root and cook it separately until tender. If ½ pound of celery is substituted, cut in small pieces.

Cool the vegetables. Peel potatoes and beets; cube these vegetables and combine them.

Mix oil and lemon juice and pour over salad. Shred the parsnip and mix in salad. Sprinkle salad with fresh dill weed.

KOHLRABI SALAD

¾ pound kohlrabi
2 apples
4 mandarins
4 tablespoons raisins
2 tablespoons chopped almonds
¾ cup yogurt
Honey, if desired
Alfalfa sprouts

Shred the kohlrabi and dice the apple. Peel the mandarin and separate in sections. Mix these 3 ingredients with raisins and chopped almonds. Mix in the yogurt; add honey to taste, if desired.

Sprinkle generously with alfalfa sprouts.

FRENCH LENTIL SALAD

1¼ cups lentils
1 vegetable bouillon cube
1 bunch parsley, chopped
2 tablespoons fresh thyme
1 tablespoon fresh, chopped lovage
1 bay leaf
2 stalks celery
5 tablespoons walnut oil
2 tablespoons herbal vinegar

Cook lentils until tender, about 30 minutes, in water with bouillon cube, chopped parsley, thyme, chopped lovage, and bay leaf.

Cut celery in paper thin slices, chop celery leaves finely, and mix with cooked lentils.

Pour an oil and vinegar dressing over salad.

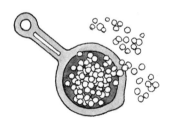

EARLY GARDEN TURNIP SALAD WITH CURRY DRESSING

2–3 firm early garden turnips
½ cup sour cream (18 percent fat content) or crème fraîche
1 tablespoon capers
Curry
Lemon juice
¼ cup almonds, shelled
Lemon balm

Slice turnips paper thin.

Mix finely cut capers with the sour cream. Add curry and lemon juice to taste and mix the turnip slices with the dressing.

Blanch the almonds, shell them, and cut them in halves. Toast them on a dry frying pan and sprinkle them on the salad with fresh, chopped lemon balm.

CHEESE SALAD

½ pound Emmenthal cheese
2–3 stalks of celery
½ head of iceberg lettuce
½ cup walnut halves
5 tablespoons walnut oil
3 tablespoons herbal vinegar
1 handful of (stinging) nettle leaves

Dice the cheese. Thinly slice the celery. Chop the leaves. Shred lettuce. Chop the walnuts. Mix all ingredients together and pour an oil and vinegar dressing over salad.

Finely chop small fresh nettle leaves and sprinkle on salad. If it is not the season for nettle, you can sprinkle with some other green leaves.

MULTICOLORED RICE SALAD

1 cup brown rice
1 green pepper
1 red pepper
1 cup cooked corn
¼ pound feta cheese
6 tablespoons olive oil
3 tablespoons herbal vinegar
1 clove of garlic
1 tablespoon fresh, chopped oregano

Rinse the rice and cook until tender, about 40 minutes. Let cool. Finely chop the peppers and mix with the rice, adding the cooked corn and crumbled feta cheese.

Shake oil and vinegar with pressed garlic and chopped oregano. Pour dressing over rice. Add a dash of salt, if desired. This salad is better if made a couple of hours before serving.

BRUSSELS SPROUTS SALAD

2 cups Brussels sprouts
4 carrots
½ cup sour cream (18 percent fat content) or crème fraîche
Lemon juice
1 bunch dill

Finely slice the Brussels sprouts and grate the carrots.

Add lemon juice to sour cream to taste and mix with freshly cut dill weed. Pour dressing over salad.

RED AND WHITE BEET SALAD

2 beets
1 thick slice celeriac or 2 stalks of celery
1 Belgian endive
1 small early garden turnip
4 tablespoons oil
2 tablespoons herbal vinegar
1 bunch parsley

Shred beets and celeriac. Cut endive into strips and dice the turnip. Mix vegetables together.

Shake oil, vinegar, and parsley together. Pour dressing over salad.

MIXED BEET SALAD

2 beets
1 jar artichoke hearts
¾ cup green beans, cut up
4 small shallots
2 tablespoons honey
1 tablespoon butter
¼ cup water
4 tablespoons olive oil
2 tablespoons herbal vinegar
Watercress

Cook beets until tender, peel and let cool, then slice thin.

Slice the artichoke hearts. Boil green beans for a couple of minutes, let cool.

Peel shallots and glaze in honey and butter. Place in a little water and steam until tender.

Pour an oil and vinegar dressing over the salad and sprinkle generously with watercress.

HORSERADISH BEETS

3 beets
½ cup yogurt
½ cup sour cream (18 percent fat content) or crème fraîche
Grated horseradish
2 tablespoons fresh, chopped lovage

Grate raw beets. Mix yogurt with sour cream, add grated horseradish and salt to taste. Toss shredded beets in dressing and sprinkle salad with finely chopped lovage.

RED CABBAGE SALAD WITH MANDARINS

8 cups finely cut red cabbage
4 tablespoons honegar (half honey, half cider vinegar)
4 mandarins
2 tablespoons flaked nuts
1 handful alfalfa sprouts

Cabbage must be cut paper thin. Toss cabbage in honegar and put in a cool place 15 minutes before serving.

Peel mandarins and separate into sections. Mix with flaked nuts and cabbage. Sprinkle top with alfalfa sprouts.

RED CABBAGE SALAD WITH CELERY

8 cups finely cut red cabbage
2 tablespoons lemon juice
1 stalk celery
1 small apple
6 dates
2 tablespoons walnut oil or corn oil
Watercress

Cabbage must be cut paper thin. Toss with lemon juice and place in a cool place 15 minutes before serving.

Thinly slice celery, and cut the apple into wedges. Coarsely chop the dates. Mix with the oil before serving. Sprinkle top with watercress.

RED CABBAGE SALAD WITH KIWI

8 cups finely cut red cabbage
4 tablespoons honegar (half honey, half cider vinegar)
1 Belgian endive
1 kiwi fruit
⅓ cup cashew nuts

Cabbage must be sliced paper thin. Toss with honegar and put in a cool place 15 minutes before serving.

Cut the endive into strips. Peel and slice the kiwi fruit. Cut each slice of kiwi in half, chop the nuts, and mix all ingredients together.

SAUERKRAUT SALAD

1 cup sauerkraut
½ pound mushrooms
½ red pepper
½ green pepper
4 tablespoons oil
2 tablespoons herbal vinegar
Fresh ginger

Mix sauerkraut with sliced mushrooms and diced peppers. Mix oil and vinegar with a little fresh, grated ginger to taste. Pour dressing over salad.

CELERIAC SALAD

½ celeriac
1 Belgian endive
½ pound blue grapes
5 tablespoons oil
2 tablespoons herbal vinegar
Alfalfa sprouts

Grate the celery root. Cut endive in strips. Seed grapes. Mix all together, adding an oil and vinegar dressing. Sprinkle generously with alfalfa or other sprouts.

COLORED CELERIAC SALAD

½ celeriac
6 tablespoons oil
2 tablespoons tamari
½ cucumber
2–3 tomatoes
1 bunch parsley

Grate the celeriac. Mix with oil and tamari. Dice cucumber and cut tomatoes into wedges; chop parsley. Mix with grated celeriac.

ITALIAN TOMATO SALAD

1 pound tomatoes
½ cucumber
1 salad onion
10 black olives
4 tablespoons olive oil
2 tablespoons herbal vinegar
1 tablespoon fresh, chopped oregano
3 tablespoons grated Parmesan cheese

Skin tomatoes, dice cucumber, and chop onion. Mix with olives, cut in half.

Shake oil and vinegar together with oregano and pour over vegetables. Sprinkle top with grated Parmesan cheese.

This salad may also be made in a Greek style, with crumbled feta cheese.

TOMATO SALAD WITH POTATOES

2 medium-size potatoes
½ pound green asparagus
2 medium-size tomatoes
5 tablespoons olive oil
2 tablespoons lemon juice
Finely chopped dill or chives

Cook the potatoes, peel, slice, and let cool. Put asparagus in boiling water and cook for 8 minutes. Cool.

Slice tomatoes and mix with potatoes and asparagus.

Pour an oil and lemon juice dressing over salad. Sprinkle top with dill or chives.

PEA SALAD

3 new potatoes, cooked
½ pound cooked asparagus
½ pound peas, shelled
4 tablespoons olive oil
2 tablespoons herbal vinegar
Fresh thyme

Peel potatoes and mix with asparagus and peas. Pour an oil and vinegar dressing over salad and sprinkle with fresh thyme.

WALDORF SALAD

4 apples
1 cup sour cream (18 percent fat content) or crème fraîche
4 stalks celery
1 cup grapes
Lemon juice
½ cup walnut halves

Coarsely dice apples. Mix at once with sour cream.

Cut the celery in thin slices. Seed grapes. Mix celery and grapes with the apples and sour cream. Add lemon juice to taste.

Coarsely chop walnuts and sprinkle over salad.

ZUCCHINI SALAD

2 leeks
2 tablespoons corn oil
1 pound zucchini
6 tablespoons corn oil
3 tablespoons herbal vinegar
1 clove garlic
2 tablespoons dill weed
½ tablespoon fresh, chopped tarragon

Finely chop the leeks, and fry them lightly in oil for 8–10 minutes. Slice the zucchini and mix with cooled leeks.

Pour a dressing of oil, vinegar, pressed garlic, and herbs over salad.

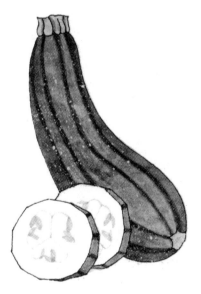

CHEESE-RADISH SALAD

1–2 bunches radishes
½ pound Emmenthal cheese
4 iceberg lettuce leaves
¾ cup sour cream or crème fraîche
½ clove garlic
4 black olives
Watercress

Slice radishes, chop the greens. Cube cheese and cut lettuce into small pieces.

Divide into 4 salad bowls or into individual portions. Top with cheese cubes and radishes.

Add pressed garlic and a pinch of salt, if desired, to sour cream. Pour dressing over salad, garnish with an olive, and sprinkle generously with watercress.

EARLY GARDEN TURNIP SALAD

2 firm early garden turnips
2 carrots
4 tablespoons olive oil
2 tablespoons lemon juice
1 teaspoon crushed thyme
1 bunch parsley

Shred turnips coarsely and grate carrots. Pour an oil and lemon juice dressing over salad. Mix crushed thyme and chopped parsley with the salad.

DRESSINGS

The salad recipes mainly call for an uncomplicated oil and vinegar dressing. But you can use dressings other than the ones suggested. For example, either orange or lemon juice may be substituted for vinegar.

There is no need to buy herbal vinegar. It is easy to make your own by soaking a few bunches of herbs such as basil, tarragon, dill, marjoram, or oregano in white, distilled vinegar for about 1 month.

The oil used for oil and vinegar dressings should always be cold-pressed. In addition to preserving taste and color, the cold-pressed oils retain most of their nutritional value.

For the more substantial salads you can use yogurt or sour cream dressings, adding flavorings in accordance with your own taste.

FRENCH DRESSING

5 tablespoons olive oil
3 tablespoons tarragon vinegar
3 tablespoons water
½ teaspoon honey
½ teaspoon crushed thyme
½ teaspoon paprika
½ teaspoon salt
½ clove garlic, pressed

Shake all ingredients together.

HERBAL DRESSING

5 tablespoons grape seed oil or corn oil
3 tablespoons herbal vinegar
3 tablespoons water
1 tablespoon chopped parsley
1 tablespoon chopped capers
1 tablespoon finely chopped pickled
  cucumber
Natural mustard
Tamari

Shake together oil, vinegar, water, chopped parsley, chopped capers, and pickled cucumber. Add a small amount of mustard and tamari to taste.

YOGURT DRESSING

¾ cup yogurt
Honey
Tarragon vinegar
Chopped fresh herbs

Add honey, vinegar, and herbs to yogurt, plus a pinch of salt if desired, all according to taste.

CURRY DRESSING

¼ cup yogurt
¼ cup sour cream (18 percent fat content)
5 tablespoons orange juice
Honey
Curry
Salt
Pepper

Mix together yogurt, sour cream, and orange juice. Add honey, curry, salt, and pepper to taste.

CHEESE DRESSING

¾ cup yogurt
Blue cheese
Chopped walnuts

Mix crumbled blue cheese with yogurt to taste. Stir dressing until smooth. Add chopped walnuts.

SOUPS

Vegetable soups are tasty and quickly prepared. In addition, you can complement the amino acids in soups by adding pre-soaked whole grains, beans, cheese, or milk products to the vegetables.

The tops of the vegetables, which are rich in vitamins and minerals, can be chopped and cooked in soups. If you have many vegetable tops, you can chop them and cook them in lots of water for 1 hour together with a chopped onion and possibly other vegetables. Drain the soup and you will get a tasty vegetable bouillon which can be frozen in portions. Mainly, cooks use the tops of parsnips, turnips, carrots, celery, beets, onions, and leeks. You can also add wild plants.

Never use the green tops of potatoes, as these contain the poison solanine.

The recipes use vegetable bouillon as a base for most of the soups. This vegetable bouillon may be either home-cooked or made with vegetable bouillon powder or cubes.

Milk, in the same amount, can be substituted for the cream and sour cream mentioned in the recipes. If you want to avoid milk products altogether, use vegetable bouillon.

The soups are meant to be a first course. If you want to serve soup as the main course, you should at least double the proportions given in the recipes. For a whole meal, serve homemade rolls or bread with the soup.

HOT CUCUMBER SOUP

1 leek
2 tablespoons oil
1 clove of garlic, pressed
2 potatoes
4½ cups vegetable bouillon
1 bouquet garni (see page 17)
1 cup milk or cream
1 cucumber
2 tablespoons fresh dill weed
2 tablespoons finely chopped spring
  onion

Finely slice the leek and sauté it in oil with the garlic. Peel and dice potatoes and add to the leek along with the bouillon and bouquet garni. Let the soup cook for 15 minutes, remove bouquet garni, then purée soup in a vegetable masher or a blender.

Return soup to pan. Dice cucumber and add to soup together with milk or cream. Cook the soup another 5 minutes.

Sprinkle with dill weed and finely chopped spring onions and serve.

COLD CUCUMBER SOUP

1 cucumber
2 teaspoons crushed mint
1 pint yogurt
Fresh mint leaves
¼ cup chopped walnuts

Thinly slice cucumber and purée in blender together with crushed mint. Mix cucumber purée in yogurt, add salt to taste, if desired.

Refrigerate until ready to serve. Serve by the portion, topping each portion with fresh, chopped mint leaves and chopped walnuts. If fresh mint leaves are not available, you can use the dried mint leaves.

MEXICAN AVOCADO SOUP

1 onion
3 tablespoons corn oil
3 tablespoons flour
4½ cups vegetable bouillon
2 avocados
1 cup cream or milk
Paprika
½ red peppper
½ green pepper

Chop onion and sauté in oil for a few minutes, add flour and hot bouillon. Cook to a smooth consistency.

Peel avocados and mash meat with a fork. Whip avocado mash into bouillon and cook the soup for 5 minutes. Pour cream into soup, and add salt to taste.

Sprinkle top with paprika and finely chopped red and green peppers.
Serve.

SPANISH AVOCADO SOUP

1 pint yogurt
1 cup milk or cream
1 cup tomato juice
2 tomatoes
1 clove of garlic, pressed
¼ cucumber
1–2 avocados
2 tablespoons lemon juice
3 tablespoons chopped chives

Mix yogurt with milk or cream and to-mato juice.

Blanch tomatoes, skin them, and cut into small pieces. Mix with pressed gar-lic and yogurt. Add diced cucumber.

Peel avocados and mash them to-gether with lemon juice and put into soup. If desired, add salt and pepper to taste. Put soup in refrigerator for a cou-ple of hours. Sprinkle with finely chopped chives just before serving.

AVOCADO-CHEESE SOUP

1 onion
3 tablespoons oil
5 tablespoons tomato purée
1 quart vegetable bouillon
3 tablespoons millet flakes
½ cup cream (13 percent fat content)
 or milk
¼ pound cream cheese
1 avocado

Chop onion and sauté in oil. Add to-mato purée, vegetable bouillon, millet flakes, and cream. Cook soup for 5 min-utes, then remove from heat and stir in the cream cheese. Warm the soup, add-ing salt and pepper to taste, if desired.

Serve cooled soup in 4 soup bowls. Place slices of peeled avocado on top of soup.

RUSSIAN BORSCH

1 onion
1 carrot
1 parsley root
2 beets, lactic acid fermented, if possible
6 cups vegetable bouillon
1 clove garlic
1 teaspoon crushed thyme
2 tablespoons tomato purée
2 tablespoons herbal vinegar
8 tablespoons sour cream (18 percent
 fat content) or crème fraîche

Chop onion. Dice carrot, parsley root, and beets. Bring bouillon to a boil, add vegetables together with pressed garlic, thyme, and tomato purée.

Cook until vegetables are tender, about 30 minutes, then purée. Put vege-table purée back in pan and add vinegar, and salt, if desired, to taste.

Top each serving with a tablespoon of sour cream.

BLENDED BROCCOLI SOUP

1 pound broccoli
2 potatoes
4½ cups vegetable bouillon
1 tablespoon fresh, chopped marjoram
½ cup cream (13 percent fat content) or milk
6 tablespoons cottage cheese
1 small celery stalk
1 clove of garlic

Finely chop broccoli. Peel and dice the potatoes. Cook vegetables about 15 minutes or until tender in bouillon together with marjoram. Purée in blender. Put purée back in the soup pot and add cream. Reheat soup, adding salt to taste if desired.

Mix finely chopped celery stalk, its leaves, and the pressed garlic with cottage cheese. Put 1 tablespoon of the cottage cheese mixture on top of each bowl of soup.

NETTLE SOUP

½ cup young nettle shoots
2 tablespoons oil
1 onion
4½ cups vegetable bouillon
1 tablespoon chopped marjoram
¾ cup milk or cream
1–2 tablespoons tomato purée

Finely chop nettle shoots and sauté in oil with finely chopped onion.

Put bouillon in pan and add chopped marjoram. Cook soup over low heat for 8 to 10 minutes. Add milk or cream, then add tomato purée and salt to taste, if desired.

You can sprinkle soup with garlic croutons, or you can serve it with creamed horseradish, which is whipped cream flavored with grated horseradish, a dash of sugar, and a little lemon juice.

GREEN SPRING SOUP

1 cup total of fresh nettle shoots, dandelion leaves, sorrel, coltsfoot, or goutweed
2 tablespoons chopped parsley
1 onion
2 tablespoons butter
4½ cups vegetable bouillon
1 cup sour cream (18 percent fat content) or crème fraîche
Kuzo, if desired
Watercress

Chop green leaves and onion and sauté in butter. Add boiling bouillon.

Cook soup for 10 minutes. Add sour cream. Add salt to taste. If the soup is too thin, thicken with a little kuzo mixed with water.

Serve sprinkled with watercress.

CARROT SOUP

1 onion
2 tablespoons oil
1 pound carrots
1 potato
4½ cups vegetable bouillon
1 cup milk
2 tablespoons sunflower seeds
1 bunch parsley

Chop onion and sauté in oil. Dice carrots and potato and add to sautéed onion. Pour bouillon vegetable and cook until they are done.

Purée vegetables in masher or blender and put back in pan. Add milk and reheat soup.

If you want to make the soup a little thicker, you can do so by adding a paste made with a little cornstarch and water.

Serve sprinkled with chopped sunflower seeds and chopped parsley.

LIGHT GREEN CABBAGE SOUP

5½ cups vegetable bouillon
1 pound cut cabbage
3 potatoes
2 celery stalks, finely grated
¼ cup chopped celery leaves
½ cup sour cream (18 percent fat content) or crème fraîche

Bring bouillon to a boil and add cabbage.

Grate unpeeled potatoes and add to the soup with the finely grated celery stalks and leaves. Cook soup for 15–20 minutes, then add sour cream. Salt and pepper may be added to taste.

ITALIAN VEGETABLE SOUP WITH PESTO

1 leek
2 potatoes
2 carrots
¼ celeriac
1 early garden turnip
1 onion
4 tablespoons oil
1 bouquet garni (see page 17)
6 cups vegetable bouillon
2 tomatoes
2 tablespoons fresh, chopped basil
1 clove garlic
¼ cup walnut halves
2 tablespoons olive oil

Finely slice the leek into strips; cut potato, carrots, celery root (celeriac), and turnip into thin strips. Chop onion.

Sauté vegetables in oil for a few minutes. Add bouquet garni and bouillon and cook for about 20 minutes.

To make pesto, a seasoning, scald the tomatoes, skin them, and cut into small pieces. Pour juice from tomatoes into soup. Grind tomatoes, basil, pressed garlic, chopped walnuts, and oil in a mortar, then stir paste until smooth.

Remove bouquet garni from soup before serving. The pesto paste is served separately with the soup, with about 1 tablespoon added to a serving.

CABBAGE SOUP

1 onion, chopped
1 green pepper, chopped
1 clove garlic
2 tablespoons oil
4½ cups vegetable bouillon
4 cups finely cut cabbage
1 bouquet garni (see page 17)
1 cup milk or cream
Cornstarch
Nutmeg
1 bunch parsley
¼ cup grated Parmesan cheese

Sauté chopped onion, peppers, and pressed garlic in oil. Pour bouillon over onions, add cabbage and bouquet garni.

Cook the soup for about 20 minutes, then add milk. Remove bouquet garni and thicken with cornstarch if a thicker soup is desired. Add ground nutmeg, salt and pepper, to taste.

Serve, sprinkled with chopped parsley and grated Parmesan cheese.

RUSSIAN CABBAGE SOUP

1 onion, chopped
1 carrot, grated
2 tablespoons oil
2 potatoes
2 cups finely cut cabbage
6 cups vegetable bouillon
2 teaspoons caraway seeds
2 tablespoons tomato purée
4 tablespoons lactic acid fermented
  mushrooms
4 tablespoons sour cream
4 tablespoons fresh dill weed

Sauté chopped onion and grated carrot in oil. Dice potatoes and add, with the cabbage, to the pan. Pour bouillon over vegetables. Add caraway seeds and tomato purée to the soup. Cook for 20 minutes.

Add mushrooms—which can be fresh—and reheat soup. Serve each portion topped with a tablespoon of sour cream or crème fraîche and sprinkled with fresh dill weed.

JERUSALEM ARTICHOKE SOUP

1 onion
1 clove of garlic
2 tablespoons oil
¾ pound Jerusalem artichokes, sliced
½ pound celeriac, diced
4½ cups vegetable bouillon
2 teaspoons crushed thyme
1 cup milk
2 ounces goat's cheese
1 tablespoon fresh, chopped sage

Sauté chopped onion and pressed garlic in oil. Add sliced artichokes and diced celeriac.

Add bouillon and thyme and cook for 15 minutes. Mash vegetables in a vegetable masher, or purée in a blender.

Put purée back in the pan and add milk. If desired, add salt and pepper to taste.

Serve sprinkled with grated goat's cheese and finely chopped sage.

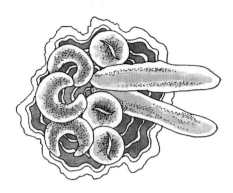

IRISH SOUP

½ cup yellow peas
¼ cup cracked wheat
Vegetable bouillon
1 onion
2 carrots
1 early garden turnip
1 stalk celery
1 bunch parsley

Soak peas and cracked wheat for 8 hours. Boil in the same water they were soaked in, adding enough bouillon to make 6 cups liquid.

Cook soup for about 1 hour. During the last 20 minutes add the finely chopped vegetables. If desired, add salt and pepper. Sprinkle with chopped parsley before serving.

CURRY SOUP

1 onion
2 carrots
2 apples
2 tablespoons oil
1–2 teaspoons curry
¼ cup brown rice
4½ cups vegetable bouillon
1 cup cream (13 percent fat content) or milk
2 tablespoons orange juice

Finely chop onion, and grate carrots and 1½ apples.

Heat oil, and add curry.

Stir onion, carrot, rice, and apple into the oil.

Add boiling bouillon and cook for 35 minutes. Add cream and salt, if desired, and possibly more curry, to taste. If the soup is too thin, thicken with a little cornstarch or kuzo mixed with water.

Grate remaining ½ apple and mix with orange juice. Sprinkle this on soup before serving.

BELGIAN ENDIVE SOUP

½ pound Belgian endives
2 celery stalks
1 onion
2 tablespoons butter
2 potatoes
1 tablespoon fresh, chopped marjoram
4½ cups vegetable bouillon
1 cup milk or cream

Cut endive and celery in fine strips. Save green celery leaves for garnish.

Sauté chopped onion, endive, and celery for 5 minutes in butter. Add grated potatoes and marjoram. Pour bouillon over vegetables and cook for 15 minutes. Add milk or cream, and reheat soup. If desired, salt and pepper may be added, to taste.

Serve sprinkled with chopped celery leaves.

POTATO-LEEK SOUP

1 onion
2 leeks
4 tablespoons oil
1 clove of garlic
4 potatoes
4½ cups vegetable bouillon
1 cup milk or cream
2 teaspoons crushed caraway seeds
1 bunch parsley
4 tablespoons chopped pumpkin seeds

Sauté chopped onion and sliced leeks in oil with pressed garlic. Dice potatoes and add with bouillon.

Cook for 10–15 minutes and pass through a vegetable masher or purée in blender. Put purée back in pan and add milk or cream. Salt and pepper may be added to taste.

Serve sprinkled with crushed caraway seeds, chopped parsley, and pumpkin seeds.

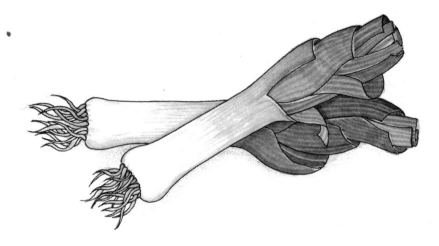

GREEN POTATO SOUP

3 potatoes
½ pound celery root, celery stalk, or celeriac
1 carrot
1 leek
4½ cups vegetable bouillon
2 tablespoons chopped chervil or spinach
1 cup sour cream or crème fraîche
2 tablespoons fresh, chopped savory

Dice potatoes, celeriac, and carrots. Slice leek. Add vegetables to boiling bouillon and cook for 15 minutes.

Add chopped chervil or spinach and crème fraîche. If desired, add salt and pepper to taste. Serve sprinkled with chopped savory.

POTATO SOUP WITH CHEESE

1 onion
2 tablespoons oil
6 potatoes
4½ cups vegetable bouillon
½ cup milk or cream
2 ounces Emmenthal cheese
4 tablespoons fresh dill

Chop onion and brown it lightly in oil. Add diced potatoes and bouillon. Cook 10–15 minutes, put through vegetable masher or purée in blender. Put purée back in the pan and bring to a boil.

Add milk or cream and grated cheese. Add salt and pepper to taste, if you desire. Sprinkle with fresh, chopped dill weed.

POTATO-CELERY SOUP

1 onion
2 tablespoons oil
3 potatoes
¾ pound celeriac or celery stalks
2 tablespoons fresh, chopped lovage
6 cups vegetable bouillon
Milk or cream
1 onion
2 tablespoons oil

Sauté chopped onion in oil. Dice potatoes and celeriac and add together with lovage and bouillon. Cook for 10–15 minutes, pass through vegetable masher or purée in blender.

Put purée back in pan and reheat. If the soup is too thick, you can add a little milk or cream. Add salt and pepper to taste.

Cut the second onion in rings. Sauté in oil until brown, and garnish soup with browned onion rings.

Potato soups can be made using other vegetables than those mentioned here. You can use parsley roots, parsnip, cabbage, cauliflower—or you can boil potatoes with herbs. You can also add ¼ to ½ cup cracked wheat (pre-soaked) to potato soups.

POTATO SOUP WITH MUSHROOMS

1 onion
2 tablespoons oil
3 potatoes
4½ cups vegetable bouillon
½ tablespoon fresh, chopped tarragon
½ pound mushrooms
½ cup milk or cream
4 tablespoons chopped parsley

Sauté chopped onion in oil. Dice potatoes and add with bouillon and tarragon. Cook for 10–15 minutes, then pass through vegetable masher or purée in blender.

Put purée back in pan. Add sliced mushrooms with milk or cream. Cook soup 5 minutes more. Add salt and pepper to taste. Serve sprinkled with chopped parsley.

TURKISH LENTIL SOUP

1 onion
1 carrot
1 stalk celery
3 tablespoons oil
½ cup lentils, soaked overnight in
  water
4½ cups vegetable bouillon
1 cup sour cream (18 percent fat content) or crème fraîche
Lemon juice
Coriander

Chop onion, grate carrot, and thinly
slice celery stalk. Save celery leaves.

Sauté vegetables in oil. Drain and add
lentils. Add bouillon. Cook for 30 minutes, then purée in blender.

Add sour cream or crème fraîche,
lemon juice, coriander, and salt and pepper to taste. Serve sprinkled with finely
chopped celery leaves.

KOHLRABI SOUP WITH CHESTNUTS

1 pound kohlrabi
1 onion
3 tablespoons oil
4½ cups vegetable bouillon
1 cup milk or cream
Paprika
½ pound chestnuts
1 bunch parsley

Sauté shredded kohlrabi and chopped
onion in oil. Pour bouillon over vegetables.

Cook for 15 minutes, then purée in
blender. Put soup back in pan, and add
milk or cream. Add paprika and a dash
of salt, to taste.

Cut a cross in the tip of each chestnut
and boil in water for about 15 minutes.
Remove shell and brown membrane.
Dice chestnuts, add to soup, and cook
for a couple of minutes.

Serve soup sprinkled with chopped
parsley.

PINK ONION SOUP

5 onions
3 tablespoons oil
4½ cups vegetable bouillon
½ cup tomato purée
1 cup cream or milk
Salt or raw cane sugar
2 slices white bread
2 tablespoons oil
1 clove garlic
1 bunch parsley

Sauté finely chopped onions in oil. Add
boiling bouillon and cook for 10 minutes. Add tomato purée and cream. You
can add salt or cane sugar to suit your
taste.

Cut bread in small cubes and toast in
oil with pressed garlic until golden.

Just before serving, sprinkle croutons
and chopped parsley on soup.

SAUERKRAUT SOUP

1 onion
2 tablespoons oil
6 ounces mushrooms
4½ cups vegetable bouillon
1 cup sauerkraut
4 whole peppercorns
1 bay leaf
½ cup cream (13 percent fat content)
Watercress

Sauté chopped onion in oil. Add chopped mushrooms. Let vegetables simmer for a couple of minutes before adding bouillon. Add sauerkraut, peppercorns, and bay leaf and cook for 10 minutes.

Remove peppercorns and bay leaf; add cream. Thicken soup if necessary. Sprinkle with watercress and serve.

CHERVIL SOUP

2 carrots
2 tablespoons butter
4 tablespoons flour
6 cups vegetable bouillon
¼ cup chervil

Dice carrots and stir in melted butter. Sprinkle flour on top and add boiling bouillon. Stir until smooth.

Cook for about 10 minutes, then add chopped chervil. You can add salt and pepper to taste. Serve at once.

COLD CREAMED VEGETABLE SOUP

1 pound leeks
6 carrots
4½ cups vegetable bouillon
1¼ cups cream (13 percent fat content) or milk
½ bunch chives

Cut leeks in thin strips, dice carrots. Bring bouillon to a boil and add vegetables.

Cook vegetables until done, then purée. Stir cream into the purée and let cool. Add salt to taste, if desired.

Serve sprinkled with finely chopped chives.

ZUCCHINI SOUP WITH SOUR CREAM

3–4 small zucchini
1 onion
3 tablespoons oil
4 tablespoons flour
4½ cups vegetable bouillon
½ cup cream or milk
5 tablespoons sour cream or crème fraîche
2 tablespoons chopped, salted almonds
Dill

Sauté sliced zucchini and chopped onion in oil. Add boiling vegetable bouillon. Sprinkle with flour. Stir constantly and cook for 5 minutes. Add cream and bring to a boil again. Add salt to taste.

Mix sour cream or crème fraîche with chopped almonds. Serve each portion with a couple of tablespoons of sour cream or crème fraîche. Sprinkle with dill weed.

CELERIAC SOUP

½ celeriac
1 onion
1 leek
Oil
1 clove garlic
4½ cups vegetable bouillon
1¼ cups cream (13 percent fat content)
 or milk
Flour
1 bunch parsley
Paprika

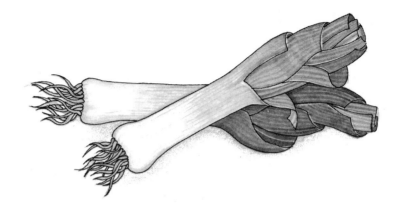

Slice and peel celeriac. Cut 1 slice into thin sticks, dice remainder.

Chop onion, and cut leek in fine strips. Sauté onion, leek, and celeriac in oil with pressed garlic. Let vegetables simmer for 5 minutes. Add bouillon.

Cook for about 15 minutes, remove celeriac sticks, then purée vegetables in blender. Put purée back into pan and add cream. If the soup is too thin, thicken it with a little flour mixed with water. Chop parsley and put in soup. Add salt to taste.

Pour soup into a bowl, put celeriac sticks on top, and sprinkle with paprika.

ALMOND SOUP

1 potato, diced
1 leek, sliced
1 tablespoon butter
4½ cups vegetable bouillon
¼ cup chopped almonds
1 cup milk or cream
Watercress

Sauté diced potato and sliced leek in butter for 5 minutes. Add bouillon and chopped almonds and cook for 15 minutes. Pass through vegetable masher or purée in blender.

Pour soup back into pan and add milk or cream. Reheat soup. If you think the soup is too thin, you can thicken by adding a little cornstarch mixed with water. Add salt to taste.

Serve sprinkled with watercress.

GREEN MISO SOUP

4½ cups water
2–3 tablespoons buckwheat miso
4 tablespoons watercress

Bring water to a boil, then remove pan from heat.

Mix miso in a little of the boiled water, then add to water in pan. Do not boil bouillon. Pour into 4 soup bowls, sprinkling 1 tablespoon watercress on each.

Miso soups can be made using many vegetables. Cut the vegetables finely, and sauté them in a little oil. Add water and cook the vegetables until tender. Then add 3 tablespoons miso to every quart of soup. Miso is not boiled since this would destroy important enzymes.

VEGETABLE ROOT SOUP

1 onion
2 tablespoons oil
2 potatoes
2 carrots
1 parsley root
¼ celeriac or celery stalk
4½ cups vegetable bouillon
2 tablespoons millet flakes
1 bouquet garni
½ cup sour cream (18 percent fat content) or crème fraîche
1 bunch parsley

Sauté chopped onion in oil. Dice vegetables and add together with the bouillon, millet flakes, and bouquet garni.

Cook vegetables until tender, about 15 minutes. Remove bouquet garni and purée soup. Pour soup back into pan and add sour cream or crème fraîche, and salt to taste.

Reheat soup. Serve sprinkled with chopped parsley.

PEPPER SOUP

1 green pepper
1 red pepper
1 yellow pepper
2 stalks celery
2 tablespoons oil
1 clove of garlic
6 cups vegetable bouillon
2 tablespoons fresh, chopped oregano
2 tablespoons chopped sunflower seeds
1 bunch parsley

Finely chop peppers. Slice celery stalks thinly and chop celery leaves. Sauté vegetables in oil with pressed garlic.

Pour boiling bouillon over vegetables, adding chopped oregano. Cook soup for about 10 minutes. Add salt to taste; thicken soup with an egg yolk if necessary.

Serve sprinkled with chopped sunflower seeds and chopped parsley.

BRUSSELS SPROUTS SOUP

1 pound Brussels sprouts
4½ cups vegetable bouillon
1 cup milk
2 tablespoons thyme
2 tablespoons butter
3 tablespoons flour
2 tablespoons almond flakes

Cut Brussels sprouts in quarters and add to boiling bouillon. Cook for about 20 minutes.

Add milk and crushed thyme. Thicken soup with a butter and flour mixture. Add salt and pepper to taste.

Toast almond flakes in ungreased frying pan and sprinkle on soup before serving.

RADISH SOUP

1 onion
2 tablespoons oil
2 tablespoons flour
4½ cups vegetable bouillon
2 bunches of radishes with leaves
½ tablespoon fresh, chopped sage
½ cup milk or cream
2 ounces Cheshire cheese or cheddar
  cheese, grated
1 bunch parsley

Sauté chopped onion in oil. Sprinkle in flour. Add boiling bouillon and stir until thickened.

Slice radishes. Finely chop the best radish leaves. Add to bouillon together with chopped sage.

Cook over low heat for 5 minutes. Add milk or cream and grated cheese. Reheat soup to a boil, adding a dash of salt to taste, if desired.

Serve sprinkled with chopped parsley.

PEA SOUP WITH CURRY CREAM

½ pound shelled peas
4½ cups vegetable bouillon
1 big potato
1 tablespoon fresh, chopped lovage
¾ cup whipping cream
About ½ teaspoon curry

Put peas in boiling bouillon. Peel potato, cut into small cubes, and add together with chopped lovage. Cook for 15–20 minutes.

Purée soup and put back in pan. Add ¼ cup whipping cream. Bring soup to a boil, adding salt to taste.

Whip the ½ cup cream, add curry to taste. Serve the whipped cream on top of the soup.

OLD-FASHIONED YELLOW PEA SOUP

¾ cup yellow peas
Vegetable bouillon
1 parsnip
½ pound Jerusalem artichokes
2 carrots
2 potatoes
½ cup finely chopped scallions or leek
1 teaspoon thyme
1 teaspoon crushed marjoram

Soak peas for 8 hours and bring to a boil in the same water together with enough bouillon to make a total of 6 cups of liquid. Cook for 35 minutes.

Dice vegetables and add to soup together with scallions (or leeks) and herbs. Cook until vegetables are done, about 25 minutes.

If desired, add salt and pepper to taste. If soup is too thick, add more water.

FIRST COURSES

First courses are rarely part of the everyday meal, which most often consists of only one main dish. First courses have, however, been included in this book because they can be made part of festive meals, and 2 or 3 of them combined may constitute a whole meal. Many of the first courses also make very good lunches.

CUCUMBERS STUFFED WITH CHANTERELLES

1 cucumber
1 onion
6 ounces chanterelles or other mushrooms
Oil
½ teaspoon thyme
2 tablespoons chopped parsley
1 egg
¼ cup granola
¼ cup whipping cream
¾ cup vegetable bouillon
Watercress

Cut cucumber lengthwise, then across. Remove seeds.

Chop onion, cut mushrooms in half and sauté both in oil. Add crushed thyme and chopped parsley. Let simmer for a few minutes.

Beat together egg with granola and cream. Mix cooled onion and mushrooms into cream mixture. Add a dash of salt and pepper to taste.

Place cucumber pieces in ovenproof dish and spoon stuffing into hollows.

Pour boiling bouillon into dish and place it in oven, preheated to 390°F, for about 25 minutes. Serve sprinkled with watercress.

Zucchini may be used instead of cucumber. In this case, use a small zucchini and cut only lengthwise.

ARTICHOKE HEARTS WITH CREAMED SPINACH

½ pound spinach
½ clove of garlic
1 shallot
½ cup cream
Nutmeg
1 jar artichoke hearts
4 lettuce leaves

Steam spinach until tender in the water on the leaves after washing. Add pressed garlic and finely chopped shallot. Add cream and let spinach simmer until the cream thickens a bit. Add ground nutmeg and salt, if desired, to taste.

Heat artichoke hearts, drain, and place on lettuce leaves. Pour creamed spinach over artichoke hearts.

ARTICHOKE HEARTS WITH LENTIL PURÉE

¼ cup lentils
1 shallot
1 bouquet garni
¼ cup sour cream or crème fraîche
1 jar artichoke hearts
4 lettuce leaves
8 slices hardboiled egg (optional)
Watercress

Wash lentils and boil together with shallot and bouquet garni for 20 minutes. Drain and remove onion and bouquet garni.

Stir lentils in the sour cream or crème fraîche and purée in blender. Add salt and pepper to taste, if desired.

Drain artichoke hearts and place on lettuce leaves. Spoon cooled purée over these.

This dish may be served hot, in which case the artichoke hearts are heated in the liquid from the jar.

Garnish with slices of hardboiled egg. Sprinkle with watercress.

ARTICHOKES
WITH GARLIC DIP

2 small artichokes
½ lemon
1 cup sour cream or crème fraîche
1–2 cloves of garlic
1 bunch parsley

Cut stalks as well as tip of leaves of arti-chokes; place in boiling water with the juice of ½ lemon and cook for 15–20 minutes. The artichokes are done when one of the middle leaves can be removed easily.

Stir cream with pressed garlic and chopped parsley. You can add a pinch of salt to the dip, if you wish.

The artichokes may be served either hot or cold. The dip is served separately.

ARTICHOKES
WITH ALMOND DIP

4 small artichokes
½ lemon
1 cup sour cream or crème fraîche
1 teaspoon crushed thyme
¼ cup chopped almonds
1 tablespoon wine vinegar
1 cup black olives

Cook artichokes as described in previous recipe.

Stir thyme, almonds, and vinegar with cream. Add dash of salt to taste.

Serve olives separately with either hot or cold artichokes.

ASPARAGUS
WITH CHEESE SAUCE

1 pound white or green asparagus
¼ pound cream cheese
¼ cup cream
Paprika
Garlic powder
2 tablespoons chopped cashew nuts or
  peanuts
4 large lettuce leaves
Watercress

Peel asparagus, if white. (Green aspara-gus is not peeled.) Cook for about 15 minutes. Drain and let cool.

Mix cream cheese with cream and 2 tablespoons boiling water until smooth. Add paprika and a pinch of garlic pow-der to taste. Add chopped nuts.

Spread asparagus on lettuce leaves, pour cheese sauce on top, and sprinkle generously with watercress.

GINGER AVOCADO

2 avocados
1 grapefruit
1 Belgian endive
4 tablespoons olive oil
½ teaspoon ground ginger
Honey or raw cane sugar
Watercress

Peel and dice avocados. Halve grapefruit, remove sections, and save juice. Cut endive in fine strips.

Make a dressing of grapefruit juice and oil. Carefully add ginger and honey, or sugar, to taste.

Mix avocado, endive, and grapefruit sections with dressing. Divide into 4 salad bowls. Serve sprinkled with watercress.

OLIVE AVOCADO

2 avocados
15 black olives
3 tablespoons chopped walnuts
4 thin lemon slices

Halve avocados and remove pits. Rub avocado edges with lemon juice.

Chop black olives finely and mix with walnuts. Spoon stuffing into avocado halves and garnish with a twisted lemon slice.

AVOCADO WITH ALMOND CREAM

2 avocados
Lemon juice
2 hardboiled eggs
4 tablespoons olive oil
2 tablespoons tarragon vinegar
3 tablespoons chopped almonds
1 teaspoon fresh, chopped marjoram
2 tablespoons chopped parsley

Halve avocados, remove pits. Rub cut edges with a little lemon juice.

Separate eggs and beat both yolks with oil and vinegar until creamy. Add finely chopped white of 1 egg, almonds, and marjoram. Add dash of salt to taste.

Pour cream into avocado halves and sprinkle with chopped parsley.

SPICED BEAN SALAD

½ cup kidney beans
½ cup garbanzo beans
1¼ cups water
1 bay leaf
1 onion
1 stalk celery
2 teaspoons crushed thyme
1–2 cloves of garlic
5 tablespoons olive oil
4 iceburg lettuce leaves
1 small green pepper

Preparation for this delicious bean salad should be started well in advance. Two days before serving, put the beans to soak overnight in 1¼ cups of water.

Next day cook the beans in the same water, adding a bay leaf, for about 50 minutes. During the last 10 minutes add finely chopped onion, celery stalk, celery leaves, and thyme.

When the beans are done, drain, and remove bay leaf. Mix in pressed garlic and olive oil. Put bean salad in refrigerator until the following day.

Put cut lettuce leaves in 4 salad bowls, add beans and garnish with finely chopped green pepper.

MUSHROOM TOAST

½ pound mushrooms
2 tablespoons oil
1 tablespoon lemon juice
4 slices toast
Paprika
1 large tomato
4 slices Emmenthal cheese
Chives

Slice mushrooms and fry in oil. Add lemon juice and let simmer for a couple of minutes.

Divide mushrooms on 4 pieces of toast, which can be buttered first. Sprinkle with paprika and place 2 slices of tomato on each piece of toast. Put cheese on top.

Preheat oven to 400 °F and put toast in oven. Heat until cheese is golden, about 20 minutes. Sprinkle with chopped chives.

BUTTER-FRIED MUSHROOMS

1 onion
2 tablespoons butter
¾ pound mushrooms
1 tablespoon lemon juice
4 iceburg lettuce leaves
2 lemon slices
Watercress

Chop onion finely and sauté in butter. Add sliced mushrooms and lemon juice. Let simmer for about 5 minutes, then spoon onto the 4 lettuce leaves.

Garnish each portion with twisted lemon slice and watercress.

Can be served with garlic-butter bread.

KOHLRABI WITH AVOCADO CREAM

2 kohlrabies
1 avocado
5 tablespoons cream
½ tablespoon fresh, chopped marjoram
2 tablespoons chopped walnuts
4 lettuce leaves

Put kohlrabies in boiling water and cook until done, about 35 minutes. Peel and cut in half. Scoop out half the meat and shred it coarsely.

Halve avocado, remove and mash pulp with a fork. Stir in cream. When smooth, add the shredded kohlrabi, chopped marjoram, and chopped walnuts. Add a dash of salt to taste, if desired.

Spoon mixture into the kohlrabi halves and serve in 4 portions on lettuce leaves.

Instead of kohlrabi, you can use early garden turnips.

STUFFED GRAPEFRUIT SHELLS

2 grapefruits
1 firm pear
¼ pound Emmenthal cheese
3 teaspoons finely chopped green pepper
Ginger
8 black olives
2 tablespoons fresh, chopped lemon balm

Halve grapefruits, remove fruit and membranes. Cut fruit into small pieces. Retain shells.

Cube both pear and cheese. Mix with grapefruit pieces and green pepper.

Add ginger to taste to a small amount of grapefruit juice and pour over mixture.

Spoon mixture into 4 grapefruit shells. Serve garnished with olives and chopped lemon balm.

VEGETABLES A LA GRECQUE

1 pound vegetables such as mushrooms, cauliflower, asparagus, zucchini, beans, broccoli (use only one)
½ cup olive oil
¾ cup water
2 tablespoons herbal vinegar
1–2 cloves of garlic
1 teaspoon crushed thyme
½ teaspoon fennel
1 teaspoon crushed basil
1 bay leaf
4 peppercorns
1 bunch parsley

Almost any kind of vegetable may be used for this Greek salad. But only one is used. These are only suggestions. Slice, cube, or halve the vegetable.

Bring oil, water, and vinegar to a boil. Add pressed garlic, crushed herbs, bay leaf, and peppercorns.

Add vegetable and cook for 8–10 minutes. Pour into a dish and refrigerate until the following day.

At serving time, drain vegetables from marinade and remove bay leaf and peppercorns. Serve salad on 4 lettuce leaves. Sprinkle with chopped parsley.

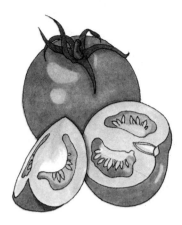

HANS ARNE'S COTTAGE CHEESE

1 cup cottage cheese
1 clove garlic
2 avocados
4 lettuce leaves
2 tomatoes
Chives

Add pressed garlic, and salt if desired, to cottage cheese according to taste.

Peel avocados and slice them. Fill avocado slices with cottage cheese and serve on 4 lettuce leaves, garnishing with tomato wedges and chopped chives.

BELGIAN ENDIVES AU GRATIN

4 large Belgian endives
3 tablespoons butter
2 tablespoons flour
About 2 cups milk
Ground nutmeg
2 ounces cheddar cheese

Put endives in boiling water and cook for 5 minutes. Drain well and put in oiled, ovenproof dish.

Stir flour into melted butter and add enough boiling milk to make a smooth sauce. Heat, and add ground nutmeg, and salt, to taste. Add grated cheddar cheese and pour sauce over endives.

Preheat oven to 425°F and bake for about 15 minutes.

PANCAKES A LA PROVENCE

½ cup whole wheat flour
4 tablespoons soy flour
1¼ cups milk
2 tablespoons olive oil
Butter for frying
1 finely chopped onion
1 large green pepper
4 medium tomatoes
1–2 teaspoons crushed basil
Olive oil

Beat wheat and soy flours with milk and oil. You can add 1 egg to the dough. Let dough rest for about 30 minutes, then bake 8–10 thin and not too large pancakes.

Sauté onion in olive oil. Cut pepper into thin rings and mix with the onion. Scald tomatoes, skin, and chop. Mix with the onion and pepper together with crushed basil. Cover and let vegetables simmer until most of the liquid has evaporated. Add salt to taste.

Put a couple of tablespoons of the vegetable mixture on each pancake. Fold pancakes and put them, partially overlapping, in an oiled, ovenproof dish. You can add a little butter on top of the pancakes before they are put in the oven. Preheat oven to 375°F and heat pancakes for about 10 minutes.

FRENCH CHEESE ENVELOPES

½ cup whole wheat flour
½ cup white flour
3 tablespoons butter
¼ pound farmer's cheese
1 small shallot, finely chopped
3 ounces Emmenthal cheese
4 tablespoons cream
Ground nutmeg

Knead the 2 flours briefly with butter and farmer's cheese. Put dough in cool place for ½ hour.

Chop shallot. Grate cheese and stir shallot and cheese with cream and a small amount of ground nutmeg.

Roll the dough out and cut in squares, about 4×4 inches. Put ½ tablespoon of cheese filling on each square. Put a little water on the edges of the squares and fold the 4 corners towards the middle, squeezing edges together.

Put the cheese envelopes on a buttered baking sheet and bake them until golden at 375 °F for 15–20 minutes.

RUSSIAN PANCAKES WITH SPINACH IN WHITE SAUCE

1 cup milk
1 package active dry yeast
½ cup wheat flour
½ cup buckwheat flour
1 egg, separated
2 tablespoons yogurt
2 tablespoons sesame seeds
Corn oil
¾ pound spinach
1 tablespoon flour
¾ cup sour cream or crème fraîche
Nutmeg

Heat the milk until warm. Mix yeast in lukewarm milk. Beat in the flour, egg yolk, yogurt, and sesame seeds. Add a dash of salt. Place dough in a warm place for 30 minutes to rise.

Whip egg white until stiff and fold in the dough. Bake 8 small pancakes in corn oil using high heat.

Steam spinach leaves tender in water that clings to them after washing. Sprinkle flour in, add cream, and heat until done. Add salt and ground nutmeg to taste.

Put a couple of tablespoons of spinach on each pancake and fold.

Try other fillings such as creamed mushrooms.

STUFFED ARABIC POCKET BREAD (PITA)

(serves 8)
1 package active dry yeast
1 cup warm water
1 teaspoon honey
1 teaspoon salt
1½ cups whole wheat flour
1½ cups white flour
1 tablespoon olive oil
1 cup cottage cheese
1 cup farmer's cheese
1 tablespoon tahini
1 clove of garlic
1 shallot
1 red pepper
1 green pepper
¼ cucumber

Mix yeast in lukewarm water with honey. Add salt and flours and knead dough thoroughly. Pour olive oil in bowl and turn dough in oil so the entire surface is lightly greased. Let the dough rise in a warm place for 1¼ hours.

Knead dough again so that the oil is absorbed. Flatten dough and fold edges towards the middle. Repeat this process a couple of times. Separate dough into 8 balls. Using a rolling pin, flatten each ball to ¼-inch thickness and 4–5 inches in diameter. Put in oven, preheated to 480 °F, and bake for 10 minutes. Make sure the oven is preheated before the breads are put in, otherwise they will not be hollow inside.

As soon as the breads are removed from the oven, put a damp cloth over them to prevent them from becoming crisp. When breads have cooled, fill them with:

Cottage cheese mixed with farmer's cheese and tahini. Stir pressed garlic and finely chopped shallot in cheese together with finely chopped peppers and cucumber. You can use other vegetables, such as tomatoes and celery stalks and leaves. Cut the breads half open and stuff with filling.

The pita breads may also be filled with other fillings such as Greek aubergine salad.

SWEET AND SOUR LEEKS

8 leeks
4 large lettuce leaves
6 tablespoons olive oil
4 tablespoons herbal vinegar
½ cup pickled cucumber
Tamari
Honey
4 tablespoons chopped raisins
1 hardboiled egg (optional)
2 tablespoons parsley

Cook leeks until just tender (8–10 minutes) and let cool. Place leeks on 4 lettuce leaves.

Mix oil and vinegar. Add diced pickled cucumber and tamari and honey to taste. Add raisins. Pour this marinade over leeks and refrigerate for a couple of hours.

Serve sprinkled with chopped egg and parsley.

LEEKS AU GRATIN

8 leeks
Oil
2 tablespoons crushed thyme
4 ounces Emmenthal cheese
4 tablespoons sesame seeds

Cook leeks until just done (8–10 minutes) and drain. Put them in an oiled, ovenproof dish. Sprinkle with thyme. Cover with sliced cheese. Sprinkle with sesame seeds.

Bake leeks for about 20 minutes in oven, preheated to 400°F.

BRUSSELS SPROUTS MOUSSE

1 pound Brussels sprouts, cleaned
2 cups vegetable bouillon
1 cup cream or milk
2 teaspoons agar-agar
1 tablespoon fresh, chopped savory
4 tomato slices
Oil
4 lettuce leaves
8 stalks cooked asparagus
½ cup sour cream (18 percent fat content) or crème fraîche
2 tablespoons finely chopped chives

Cut Brussels sprouts across stem and put in boiling bouillon. Cook over low heat for 15 minutes. Remove saucepan from heat and add cream. Purée in blender and put purée back in pan.

Mix agar-agar with a little water and add to purée. Reheat purée to boiling. Add chopped savory.

Put tomato slices in 4 oiled salad bowls. Divide the mousse into the bowls and refrigerate for a couple of hours.

Turn the mousse upside-down on 4 lettuce leaves. Top each with 2 asparagus stalks. Mix sour cream or crème fraîche with finely chopped chives and pour over each portion.

This mousse can be made with cauliflower, broccoli, celery, and other vegetables.

RUSSIAN BEETS

2 beets
6 new potatoes
4 large lettuce leaves
6 tablespoons oil
3 tablespoons herbal vinegar
1 hardboiled egg (optional)
Dill weed

Cook beets and potatoes separately until done. Peel and let cool, then dice.

Distribute vegetables on lettuce leaves and pour on an oil and vinegar dressing. Garnish with chopped egg and dill weed.

STUFFED BEETS WITH DILL SAUCE

4 beets
¼ pound cream cheese
4 tablespoons raisins
4 tablespoons chopped walnuts
1 teaspoon crushed thyme
1 onion
Corn oil
1 cup yogurt
1 bunch dill

The beets should be round, but a little flat in shape. Put in boiling water and cook until not quite done, about 35 minutes.

Skin the beets and partially hollow

them, carefully removing about ⅓ of each beet with a spoon. Half of the beet removed must be finely chopped, the rest may be used in a salad.

Stir cream cheese until smooth. Pour boiling water over raisins and let soak for 5 minutes before mixing with the cream cheese, chopped beet, chopped walnuts, crushed thyme, and finely chopped onion.

Put the hollowed beets in a greased ovenproof dish, fill beets with cream cheese mixture and top with a little oil. Place in oven, preheated to 350 °F, for 15 minutes.

To make the sauce, mix farmer's cheese with finely chopped dill weed. Add salt to taste, if desired.

Stuffed beets may be served either hot or cold. In addition to the dill sauce, French bread and a green salad may be served.

BEET OVERTURE

2–3 beets
16 green olives
2 tablespoons capers
5 tablespoons olive oil
2 tablespoons herbal vinegar
1 small shallot
4 iceburg lettuce leaves

Cook beets until done, skin, and let cool. Cut in thin slices and mix with sliced olives and chopped capers.

Mix oil and vinegar with finely chopped shallot and pour dressing over leeks. Refrigerate salad for a couple of hours.

Serve beet salad on lettuce leaves, garnished with 2 chopped hardboiled eggs (optional).

SUNSHINE BREAD

4 slices rye or pumpernickel bread
Butter
6 ounces Gorgonzola cheese
4 large onion rings
4 egg yolks
4 tablespoons chopped radishes
Chives

Toast bread, butter it, and top with Gorgonzola cheese. Place a large onion ring in the middle of each slice of cheese. Separate eggs carefully and put a yolk inside each onion ring. Save the egg whites for another dish.

Garnish with chopped radishes and finely cut chives.

NEAPOLITAN SPAGHETTI

2 onions
2 tablespoons oil
2 cloves of garlic
4 ripe tomatoes
2 teaspoons crushed thyme
1 bay leaf
½ cup tomato purée
½–1 cup water
½ pound soya spaghetti or whole
   wheat spaghetti
1 tablespoon oil
Grated Parmesan cheese (optional)

Chop onions and sauté in oil with pressed garlic.

Scald tomatoes, peel, and cut in small pieces. Put in frying pan with crushed thyme and bay leaf. Add tomato purée and water and let the sauce simmer for 8–10 minutes. Add salt to taste, if desired.

Add oil to water and bring to a boil. Add spaghetti and cook for about 12 minutes.

Drain spaghetti well and pour sauce over it. Sprinkle with grated Parmesan cheese (optional).

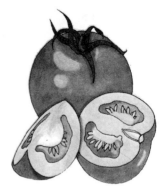

TOMATO CROUTONS

4 slices whole grain white bread
2 tablespoons butter
4 tomatoes
½ tablespoon fresh, chopped tarragon
2 ounces Emmenthal cheese

Fry bread in butter.

Slice tomatoes and put on fried bread, sprinkle with tarragon and grated cheese.

Bake tomato croutons in oven, preheated to 400°F, until cheese is golden.

TOMATOES WITH CREAMED HORSERADISH

4 large beefsteak tomatoes
½ cup whipping cream
Shredded horseradish
½ cup cooked brown rice
2 tablespoons chopped parsley
Lemon juice
4 lettuce leaves

Slice off tops of tomatoes and retain as lids. Remove the pulp.

Whip cream until stiff and add horseradish to taste. Fold in cooked rice, chopped parsley, and a little lemon juice. Fill tomatoes with this mixture, top with "lid," and serve on lettuce leaves.

You can also fill tomatoes with creamed avocado, used for cheese puffs.

WAX BEANS WITH OLIVES

1 pound wax beans
1 shallot, chopped finely
6 tablespoons olive oil
3 tablespoons herbal vinegar
1 tablespoon fresh, chopped basil
4 lettuce leaves
10 stuffed olives

Cook beans in boiling water for 4 minutes. Drain and let them cool.

Chop shallot and basil and mix with oil and vinegar. Pour dressing over beans and refrigerate for a couple of hours.

Serve beans on lettuce leaves, garnishing with sliced stuffed olives.

OLIVE EGGS

4 hardboiled eggs
1 Belgian endive
1 large tomato
4 large lettuce leaves
¾ cup sour cream or crème fraîche
Paprika
16 stuffed olives
Watercress

Chop eggs, cut endive in strips, and cut tomato into small pieces. Mix together and spoon onto lettuce leaves.

Add salt and paprika to the sour cream or crème fraîche to taste. Pour dressing over the salad and garnish with sliced stuffed olives and watercress.

MAIN COURSES

The main meal of the day may be a raw vegetable salad, a dish of cooked vegetables with side dishes, or a combination of several minor dishes.

With main dishes, you may serve vegetable side dishes such as raw vegetables, rice, beans, millet, grains, pasta, or bread.

Artichoke

The artichoke is not a vegetable, but the flower of a thistle. The heart of the flower and the outermost petals are eaten.

The artichoke originates from southern Europe, where it has been used for centuries because of its cleansing effect in folk medicine. It contains proteins, vitamins A, B, and C, plus several minerals and inulin, which is beneficial to the liver.

Cook artichokes in water with a little lemon juice to preserve their color.

ARTICHOKES AU GRATIN

4 large artichokes
Lemon juice
1 onion, finely chopped
Oil
½ pound mushrooms, chopped
2 tablespoons lemon juice
1 cup cream
Cornstarch
12 stuffed olives
2 ounces grated Parmesan cheese

Cut off the artichoke stalks and tips of leaves. Put artichokes in boiling water with a little lemon juice (3 tablespoons to each quart of water) and cook for 35–40 minutes. Artichokes are cooked when one of the leaves of the middle part is easily removed. Remove outermost leaves and carefully remove the fibers with a spoon.

Chop onion and sauté in a small amount of oil. Add chopped mushrooms and lemon juice. Let simmer for a couple of minutes, then add cream. If you use whipping cream, let it cook until it thickens, otherwise thicken the cream with a little cornstarch mixed with water. Add sliced stuffed olives and salt and pepper to taste.

Spoon sauce over artichokes, sprinkle with grated cheese, and put in the oven, preheated to 390 °F, for about 20 minutes.

Serve with whole grain French bread or rolls.

ARTICHOKES
WITH EGG FILLING

4 large artichokes
Lemon juice
2 hardboiled eggs
8 tablespoons lactic acid fermented
   beets, diced, or 4 pickled beet slices
2 tablespoons capers
1 cup sour cream or crème fraîche

Cook artichokes and make them "hollow" as described in the previous recipe.

Split hardboiled eggs lengthwise and put ½ egg on each artichoke. If you use pickled beet slices, dice them. Chop capers. Mix beets and capers in the cream and spoon dressing over the artichokes.

Serve either hot or cold and with whole grain bread.

ASPARAGUS-POTATOES

4 potatoes
1 pound green asparagus
2 tablespoons chopped nuts
1 cup cream
2 eggs
1 bunch parsley
2 ounces Emmenthal cheese
3 tablespoons crushed granola

Cook potatoes until almost done, then peel and slice them.

Cut a small piece off the butt of the asparagus, tie all into a bunch with cotton string, and cook in boiling water for 8 minutes. Drain. The green asparagus does not need to be peeled.

Grease a round, ovenproof dish (or a pie pan). Arrange potato slices in bottom and top with a circle of asparagus. Sprinkle chopped nuts on top.

Beat together cream with egg and chopped parsley and pour over vegetables. Sprinkle top with grated cheese and granola.

Put the dish in the oven, preheated to 390 °F, until top is light brown, about 20–25 minutes.

Instead of potatoes, you may use rice.

Aubergines

Aubergines are also known as eggplants. The large purple fruit originated in India, and has been grown in Denmark during recent years.

Aubergines are not very nutritious, but have a pleasant taste, and they combine well with many other vegetables.

AUBERGINES AU GRATIN

3–4 aubergines
Oil
4 tomatoes
½ cup tomato paste
1 tablespoon crushed basil
½ cup cream or milk
Soya flour
Salt and cane sugar
½ pound grated Emmenthal cheese

Cut aubergines in approximately ½-inch slices lengthwise. Fry them in oil until almost tender. You will use less oil if you cover frying pan while frying aubergines. You can also add a small amount of water.

Scald tomatoes, peel them, and cut into small pieces. Add tomato paste, crushed basil, and cream. The sauce may be thickened, if needed, with a little flour mixed with water. Add salt and sugar to taste.

Put a layer of the tomato mixture on the bottom of an ovenproof dish, then a layer of aubergine slices sprinkled with ⅓ of the grated cheese. Repeat layers and top with sauce and remainder of the grated cheese.

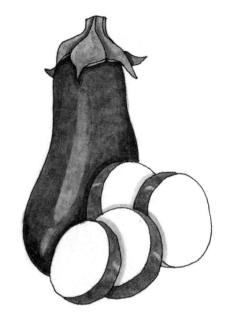

Put dish in oven, preheated to 390 °F, until cheese is golden, about 30 minutes.

A salad made with iceberg lettuce, green peppers, and cucumbers with a garlic dressing is a good accompaniment to aubergines. Top it off with homemade whole wheat bread, and you have a satisfying and nutritious meal.

AUBERGINES WITH BEAN FILLING

3–4 aubergines
1 onion
Oil
2 teaspoons crushed thyme
½ teaspoon crushed tarragon
¼ cup chopped hazelnuts
1 pound green beans
8 tablespoons grated cheese
1 cup vegetable bouillon

Halve aubergines and scoop out meat, leaving only ¼ inch in shell. Remove seeds and chop meat finely.

Sauté chopped onion in oil with chopped aubergine meat and crushed herbs. Let simmer for 5 minutes. Add chopped nuts.

Put beans in boiling water and cook for 5 minutes. Drain well before spooning into aubergine shells. Place shells close together in an ovenproof dish.

Spread sautéed vegetables over the beans and sprinkle grated cheese on top. Pour boiling bouillon in the dish and cover with foil.

Put aubergines in oven, preheated to 390 °F, for 50–60 minutes. Remove foil during last 20 minutes.

Serve cooked millet or rice with this dish.

AUBERGINES WITH RICE STUFFING

4 aubergines
¾ cup brown rice
1 teaspoon turmeric
1½ cups water
¼ cup olive oil
15 green olives
4 tablespoons chopped walnuts
1 bunch parsley
1 onion, chopped
1 cup water
1 vegetable bouillon cube
½ cup chopped celery leaves
1 cup milk

Put aubergines in boiling water and cook for 5 minutes. Halve and spoon out ¾ of the meat. Dice the meat that has been removed, removing any seeds.

Put rice and turmeric in 1½ cups water. Cook until done, about 40 minutes. When the rice has cooled a little, mix it with olive oil, sliced olives, chopped walnuts, and chopped parsley. Add a dash of salt to taste.

Sauté chopped onion in oil. Add diced aubergine with 1 cup water, bouillon cube, and chopped celery leaves. Cook for 15 minutes, then purée in blender. Put purée back in pan and add enough milk to give a sauce-like consistency. Add salt and pepper to taste.

Pour purée into ovenproof dish. Put hollowed aubergines in the dish and fill with the rice mixture.

Put dish in oven, preheated to 390 °F, and cook until the aubergines are tender, about 50 minutes.

Serve with a salad made with lettuce, tomato, and cucumber slices.

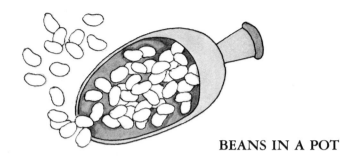

BEANS IN A POT

1 cup pinto beans
4 onions
4 tablespoons oil
1 clove garlic
2 aubergines, diced
2 teaspoons crushed thyme
1 cup milk or cream
Kuzo or cornstarch
1 bunch parsley

Rinse beans and soak overnight. Cook in the same water until tender, about 60 minutes.

Chop onions and sauté in oil with pressed garlic. Add diced aubergines and thyme. Let simmer in covered frying pan for about 15 minutes.

Drain cooked beans and add to frying pan. Add milk or cream. Thicken with either a little kuzo or cornstarch mixed with a little water.

Serve garnished with chopped parsley.

This can be served with baked potatoes or rice.

Cannelloni

Cannelloni is a popular Italian dish which consists of tubes of pasta filled with finely cut vegetables or cottage cheese. Cannelloni is baked in the oven with either tomato sauce or Bechamel sauce, and is usually sprinkled with grated cheese.

If the cannelloni is not cooked first, it must be completely covered with sauce when baked; otherwise it will not soften. Check box to see whether it is cooked.

VENETIAN CANNELLONI

1 fennel
2 onions, chopped finely
Oil
2 cloves garlic
½ pound mushrooms, diced
1 zucchini, diced
2 celery stalks, thinly sliced
1–2 teaspoons ground oregano
4 tomatoes
½ cup milk or water
2 teaspoons crushed basil
16–20 cannelloni (they are purchased in half-pound boxes)
½ pound mozzarella cheese, sliced

Split fennel into 4 parts, put in boiling water, and cook until done, 8–10 minutes. Drain water, which can be saved to make the tomato sauce.

Sauté chopped onions in oil with pressed garlic. Add diced mushrooms and zucchini. Add thinly sliced celery stalks, and chopped celery leaves.

Cover and simmer for 6–8 minutes, then sprinkle with oregano. Add chopped, cooked fennel.

To make tomato sauce, scald tomatoes, peel, and slice them. Cut into small pieces and cook with a little water (in which the fennel was cooked) or with milk for about 5 minutes. Add crushed basil and thicken with a little flour mixed with water. You can add salt and cane sugar to taste.

Pour ¾ of the tomato sauce into an ovenproof dish. Fill cannelloni with vegetable mixture and place close together in the sauce. Pour rest of the tomato sauce over the cannelloni. Top with sliced cheese.

Bake in oven, preheated to 390 °F, until cheese is golden, about 30 minutes.

A big bowl of lettuce with garlic dressing makes an excellent finishing touch to this dish.

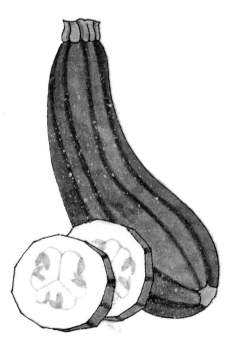

DELICIOUS CHEESE CANNELLONI

16–20 cannelloni
½ pound spinach
1 clove garlic
¾ pound cottage cheese
½ pound Emmenthal cheese
Nutmeg
1 onion
Oil
4 tomatoes
½ cup tomato paste
Salt and cane sugar to taste
2 tablespoons butter
2 tablespoons flour
1¼ cups milk

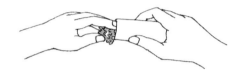

Cheese cannelloni is baked in 2 kinds of sauce: a tomato sauce base and a Bechamel sauce cover. It is a very delicious dish, so it will be wise to make plenty of it.

Check box to see if cannelloni needs to be cooked.

Steam spinach until done in the water that clings to the leaves after washing. Add pressed garlic. When cooked spinach has cooled a little, mix in the cottage cheese. Add half of the grated Emmenthal cheese and ground nutmeg, plus salt to taste.

To make the tomato sauce, chop onion and sauté in oil. Scald tomatoes, peel, and cut into small pieces. Mix with sautéed onion and the tomato paste. Let simmer over low heat for a couple of minutes. Add salt and cane sugar to taste.

To make the Bechamel sauce, melt the butter, mix in the flour, and moisten with milk. Add ground nutmeg and salt to taste.

Pour tomato sauce into ovenproof dish. Pack cannelloni with vegetable mixture and place close together in the tomato sauce. Pour Bechamel sauce over cannelloni and sprinkle remainder of the grated cheese on top.

Put dish in oven, preheated to 390°F, until cheese is golden, about 30 minutes.

Any kind of lettuce salad will go well with this dish.

MADS' FENNEL AU GRATIN

4 fennels
2 tablespoons butter
4 tablespoons flour
2½–3 cups fennel water and milk
½ pound Emmenthal cheese
Nutmeg

Cut the 4 fennels in half. Remove stalks and green parts, but save the leaves. Put fennel halves in boiling water and cook for about 10 minutes. Drain well and put round side up in an oiled, ovenproof dish.

Melt butter; mix flour, fennel water, and milk to make a sauce. Grate cheese and put ¾ of it in the sauce. Add nutmeg and salt to taste. Add chopped green fennel leaves to sauce.

Pour sauce over fennel and sprinkle remainder of cheese on top. Put dish in oven, preheated to 390°F, until top is golden, about 25 minutes.

Serve a green salad and baked sesame potatoes with this dish.

CREOLE SALAD

About 2 pounds vegetables, for example, mushrooms, celery, green and red peppers, cauliflower, peas, tiny new carrots, cucumbers, kohlrabi, radishes
¾ cup olive oil
1 shallot
½ teaspoon cayenne pepper
½ teaspoon pepper
½ teaspoon turmeric
2 teaspoons ground caraway

Creole salad may be served either as a main dish or in smaller portions as a salad or a side dish.

Start preparation of this salad the day before you want to serve it. Cut vegetables in slices or small cubes. Blanch finely cut celery, peppers, cauliflower, peas, carrots, and kohlrabi for a couple of minutes in boiling water. Do not blanch mushrooms, cucumber, or radishes.

Arrange vegetables decoratively in a large dish.

Sauté finely chopped onion and herbs in olive oil. Pour dressing over vegetables, cover, and refrigerate until the fol-

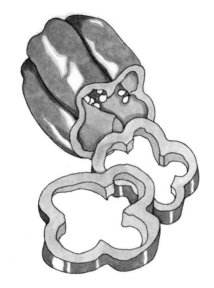

lowing day. Stir vegetables a couple of times.

All kinds of vegetables, according to season, may be used for this salad. The above are merely suggestions.

You may serve the salad with sour cream or crème fraîche mixed with a choice of herbs or pressed garlic. Whole grain French bread can also be served with this dish, or you may prefer baked potatoes.

FENNEL IN MUSHROOM SAUCE

4 fennels
½ pound mushrooms
1 green pepper
Oil
¾ cup milk
¾ cup fennel cooking water
Wheat flour

Cut the 4 fennels in half. Remove stalks, but save the green leaves. Put fennel pieces in boiling water and cook for about 15 minutes.

Slice mushrooms and dice green pepper. Sauté in oil for a few minutes. Pour milk and fennel water over vegetables and thicken with a little flour mixed with water. Chop the fennel leaves and put in the sauce. Heat sauce, to which you may add salt to taste.

At serving time pour sauce over fennel halves.

You may serve potatoes or French bread and salad with this dish.

Okra

Okra came from Africa. It is an interesting vegetable, which can sometimes be purchased fresh. It is also sold in cans. Okra can be used in soups and sauces with a slight thickening effect, or it can be fried in oil. It is never eaten raw.

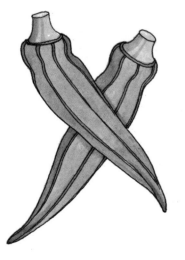

AFRICAN VEGETABLES WITH COUSCOUS

½ cup garbanzo beans
1 onion
Oil
2 cloves garlic
½ pound mushrooms
3 carrots
1 aubergine (eggplant)
1 zucchini
4 tomatoes
½ pound okra (or green beans)
2 tablespoons tamari
1 teaspoon red pepper
1 teaspoon coriander
1 teaspoon paprika
1 teaspoon cardamom
½ pound couscous

Rinse garbanzo beans and soak overnight. Cook in same water for 30 minutes.

Sauté onion wedges in oil with pressed garlic. Add whole mushrooms. Finely slice carrots, aubergine, and zucchini. Dip tomatoes in boiling water for 30 seconds, put in cold water for 60 seconds, peel, and cut into little pieces. Use okra whole; if you use green beans, cut them in half. Put all vegetables in a pan with the half-cooked garbanzo beans and 1 cup water. Add tamari and herbs.

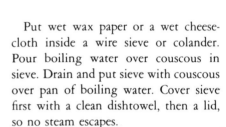

Put wet wax paper or a wet cheesecloth inside a wire sieve or colander. Pour boiling water over couscous in sieve. Drain and put sieve with couscous over pan of boiling water. Cover sieve first with a clean dishtowel, then a lid, so no steam escapes.

Couscous will now steam until done, while vegetables simmer over low heat for about 40 minutes. Watch that all the water does not evaporate from pan of vegetables. If it does, add a little more water, or a little tomato juice or tomato sauce.

Add salt to the vegetables to taste.

Serve vegetables on a round dish surrounded by the couscous. If couscous is unavailable, serve cooked rice instead.

GREEN VEGETABLE PIE

(serves 5–6 persons)
¼ cup mung beans
1 cup water
1 vegetable bouillon cube
1 package active dry yeast
1 teaspoon honey
6 tablespoons olive oil
¾ cup buckwheat flour
¾ cup whole wheat flour
¾ cup wheat germ
1 cup all-purpose flour
1 pound broccoli
5 ounces pickled cucumber
4 ounces Emmenthal cheese
2 teaspoons ground oregano
Oil

Rinse mung beans and soak for a couple of hours. Cook them in the same water until done, 30 minutes.

To make the dough, dissolve vegetable bouillon cube in water at 105–115 °F in a large bowl. Mix in yeast, let stand 3–5 minutes, then add honey, olive oil, buckwheat flour, whole wheat flour, and wheat germ. Knead in all-purpose wheat flour, a little at a time. Let dough rise in a warm place for 1 hour.

Cut broccoli in small pieces and steam in a little water until done. Chop cucumber and slice cheese.

Divide the dough in 2 parts and roll out flat. Put 1 part in a greased pie pan. Spoon the cooked mung beans over dough. Top with chopped cucumber and broccoli. Sprinkle with oregano and a dash of salt. Top with sliced cheese.

Cover with second piece of dough, pressing it firmly around the edges. Cut a small cross in the crust to release steam. Brush the crust with oil or a beaten egg. Bake in oven, preheated to 390 °F, for 30–40 minutes. Serve a colorful salad with this dish.

FETTUCINE WITH BRUSSELS SPROUTS SAUCE

½ pound chestnuts
1¼ pounds Brussels sprouts
2 tablespoons butter
4 tablespoons flour
About 2 cups water (in which Brussels sprouts were cooked)
2 teaspoons crushed thyme
Nutmeg
1 bunch parsley
¾ pound fettucine
2 tablespoons butter

Cut a cross in the tip of each chestnut. Put them in boiling water and cook for 15 minutes. Remove shell and brown membrane.

Cook Brussels sprouts until just done.

Melt 2 tablespoons butter, mix in flour and water from Brussels sprouts to make a sauce. Add crushed thyme, ground nutmeg, and salt to taste. Heat sauce.

Add cut chestnuts and Brussels sprouts to sauce together with chopped parsley.

Cook fettucine in boiling water for 12 minutes. Drain and place in a dish. Stir remaining butter in fettucine until butter is melted and fettucine is well coated. Make sure sauce is very hot before pouring over fettucine.

WHOLE WHEAT
AND VEGETABLE CASSEROLE

1½ cups whole wheat grains
1 onion
Oil
1 pound beets
4 carrots
1 parsley root
½ pound mushrooms
Thyme
1 bunch parsley
4 tablespoons sesame seeds

Rinse wheat grains and pour 3 cups boiling water over them. Let soak overnight.

The next day, chop onion and sauté in oil. Dice beets, carrots, and parsley root and add to sautéed onion. Pour in wheat grains and water, cover, and let simmer over low heat for 50 minutes. During the last 5–10 minutes, add sliced mushrooms and crushed thyme. Add water if needed.

Salt and pepper can be added to taste. Serve sprinkled with chopped parsley and toasted sesame seeds.

STUFFED CABBAGE LEAVES
A LA HARLEKIN

1 small cabbage
¾ cup brown rice
1 onion
Oil
1 green pepper
1 red pepper
½ cup corn
4 ounces cream cheese
1 bunch dill

Put cabbage head in boiling water. Carefully remove 16–18 leaves as they become tender. Cook remainder of cabbage until done, saving the water for the sauce.

Finely chop 1 cup of the center of the cabbage. Remaining cabbage can be used with a white sauce for another meal. Cook rice until tender, about 40 minutes. Finely chop onion and sauté in oil. Add chopped peppers. Cook corn for a couple of minutes and mix with onion and peppers.

When rice is cooked, mix in the sautéed vegetables, chopped cabbage, and cheese. Cut half of the dill very fine and add it, with a dash of salt to taste.

Put 1–2 tablespoons of this mixture on each cabbage leaf. Fold leaves and put the stuffed leaves in an ovenproof dish. Heat in 250 °F oven for 10–15 minutes.

The water in which the cabbage was cooked can be thickened to make a sauce, to which can be added dill weed to taste. You can serve potatoes or bread with this dish.

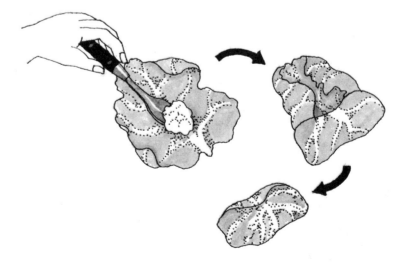

BAKED COTTAGE CHEESE DISH

1 onion
4 leeks
2 carrots
3 tablespoons oil
2 cups cottage cheese
1 bunch parsley
½ cup crushed granola or breadcrumbs
About 1 cup milk
2 eggs
1 tablespoon fresh, chopped marjoram

Chop onion, slice leeks, and coarsely grate carrots. Sauté vegetables in oil for about 5 minutes. Let them cool, then mix them with the cottage cheese. Add chopped parsley, granola, milk, eggs, and chopped marjoram. Stir and add salt and pepper to taste.

Grease ovenproof dish, sprinkle with granola, then pour mixture into dish. Put in oven, preheated to 390 °F, until top is golden, about 35 minutes.

Serve a salad and celery-walnut patties with this dish.

CHANTERELLE SOUFFLÉ

1 cup dry soya noodles (or whole wheat noodles)
Corn oil
1 onion
½ pound chanterelles, or other mushrooms
3 tablespoons butter
3 tablespoons cornstarch
1 cup milk
1 teaspoon crushed mint
½ teaspoon crushed sage
½ pound farmer's cheese
2 tablespoons grated Parmesan cheese
Salt (optional)
3 eggs, separated

Put soya noodles in boiling water with ½ tablespoon oil, and cook for 8 minutes. Drain noodles and rinse with cold water. Let noodles drain well.

Sauté finely chopped onion in oil.

Clean chanterelles thoroughly in salted water, rinse, and drain. Cut in half and mix with the sautéed onion. Let simmer over low heat for 5 minutes.

Bring butter, cornstarch, and milk to a boil while stirring. Add crushed mint and sage.

When sauce has cooled slightly, stir in farmer's cheese and grated Parmesan cheese. Beat in 3 egg yolks, one at a time. Cut up noodles and add to sauce. Add salt to taste.

Whip egg whites well and fold carefully into the sauce. Put soufflé in ovenproof dish with straight sides. Remember, it will rise to double size.

Bake soufflé in oven, preheated to 350 °F, for 35–40 minutes and serve at once.

Potatoes are served with this dish. Instead of boiled or baked, make a potato salad.

GREEN POTATO GRATIN

7 average-sized potatoes
1 onion
4 tablespoons oil
4 tablespoons flour
3 cups milk or vegetable bouillon
1 cup chopped kale or spinach
Nutmeg
3 eggs, separated

Boil potatoes until almost done. Peel and slice.

Sauté chopped onion in oil until golden. Add flour and mix in milk or vegetable bouillon. Add chopped kale or spinach and heat in sauce for about 5 minutes. Add ground nutmeg and salt to taste.

Remove pan from heat and stir in egg yolks. Mix in potato slices. Whip egg whites until stiff and fold carefully in the sauce.

Pour mixture into a greased, ovenproof dish with enough room for mixture to rise. Bake until golden in oven, preheated to 300 °F, for about 45 minutes.

CELERY POTATOES

1 celeriac
6 potatoes
Oil
1 cup chopped celery leaves
4 cups milk and celery water
½ cup sesame seeds

Slice and peel celeriac. Put in boiling water and cook for 4 minutes.

Thinly slice potatoes.

Cut celeriac slices into sticks and put into a greased, ovenproof dish. Sprinkle chopped celery leaves on top and cover with potato slices. Pour milk, or the water in which the root was cooked, or a mixture of both, over the vegetables.

Sprinkle sesame seeds on top and put dish in oven, preheated to 390 °F, for 45-50 minutes.

Whole grain bread and a salad can be served with this dish.

ALMOND POTATOES

8 potatoes
1 pound carrots
6 tablespoons butter
1 cup almonds

Cut potatoes into thin sticks. Slice carrots paper thin.

Stir julienne potatoes in 4 tablespoons of melted butter for about 5 minutes. Put potatoes aside. Put carrot slices in the rest of the butter and cook for 5 minutes.

Put half of the julienne potatoes in a greased, ovenproof dish. Finely chop almonds and sprinkle on top of potatoes. Add carrot slices. Top with remainder of potatoes.

Press vegetables together and put dish in oven, preheated to 390 °F, for 45-50 minutes.

Serve boiled barley grains, rissoles, a couple of salads, or baked vegetables with this dish.

POTATO AND PARSNIP AU GRATIN

7 average-sized potatoes
2 parsnips
2 onions
Oil
1 tablespoon fresh chopped sage
  or 1 teaspoon dried sage
1 bunch parsley
½ cup sunflower seeds
3 cups milk

Scrub potatoes and parsnips until clean, but do not peel or scrape them. Cut into paper thin slices, in food processor, if available.

Cut onions in rings and fry in oil until golden.

Put half of the potato slices in a greased, ovenproof dish. Add sliced parsnip and fried onion. Sprinkle with chopped parsley and chopped sage, then with sunflower seeds. Top with remaining potato slices. A dash of salt and pepper may be added, if desired.

Press the vegetables down and pour milk over them. Put dish in oven, preheated to 375 °F, until vegetables are done, about 50 minutes.

You can serve one or two salads with this dish.

Chestnuts

Chestnuts are used in many dishes in countries surrounding the Mediterranean where venders sell roasted chestnuts all winter at every street corner.

Chestnuts are available from September until well into the winter, and in many ways they are an excellent variation in vegetarian cooking. Not only do they taste good, but in relation to their calorie content of about 190 calories per 100 grams (3½ ounces), they are rich in nutrition. Chestnuts contain proteins, vitamins A, B, and C, as well as a number of minerals and trace minerals.

BAKED CHESTNUTS WITH CHEESE

1½ pounds chestnuts
1½ pounds Brussels sprouts
2 tablespoons butter
3½ tablespoons flour
2½ cups Brussels sprouts cooking water
4 tablespoons chopped nuts
1½ cups grated Emmenthal or cheddar cheese

Cook and peel chestnuts as described in following recipe. Cook Brussels sprouts in boiling water for 10 minutes. Drain and place in a greased, ovenproof dish with the chestnuts.

Melt butter, add flour to make a roux, then add hot vegetable water and stir to a smooth consistency. Add a pinch of salt and pepper to taste. Add chopped nuts.

Pour sauce over vegetables. Sprinkle top with grated cheese. Put dish in oven, preheated to 375 °F, and cook until cheese is golden, about 20 minutes.

Serve red cabbage salad with this dish.

AUTUMN CASSEROLE

1 pound chestnuts
1 pound carrots
2 tablespoons honey
¾ cup water
1 pound firm pears
½–1 teaspoon ginger
1 cup brown rice
2 cups yogurt
Mango chutney

Cut a cross in the tip of each chestnut. Put them in boiling water and cook for 15 minutes. Remove shell and brown membrane.   Cut carrots lengthwise in quarters and then cut into 2-inch pieces. Let carrots simmer in the honey for a few minutes. Add water and cook the carrots over low heat for another 10 minutes.

Cut pears in wedges and mix with carrots and ginger. If water has evaporated, add a little more. Let carrots and pears simmer for about 10 minutes, or until they are done. Add chestnuts during the last 5 minutes.

For a richer casserole, use half yogurt and half sour cream.

Cook rice until tender, about 40 minutes. Add mango chutney to yogurt to taste. Rice and sauce are served separately with this dish.

STUFFED CABBAGE LEAVES WITH CHESTNUT FILLING

½ pound dried chestnuts
1 small cabbage
½ cup farmer's cheese
¼ cup granola
½ cup milk or cream
2 tablespoons fresh, chopped lovage
1¼ cups cabbage cooking water
4 tablespoons honey
2 tablespoons butter

Soak chestnuts in lots of water for about 8 hours. Cook in the same water until tender, about 15 minutes, and drain.

Put cabbage head in boiling water. Carefully remove 16–18 outer leaves when they are tender, and cook the rest of the cabbage head until done. Save the water. Finely chop 1½ cups of the cabbage head.

Coarsely chop half of the chestnuts and mix with farmer's cheese together with the chopped cabbage, granola, milk or cream, and chopped lovage. Add salt to taste, if desired.

Put 1–2 tablespoons filling on each cabbage leaf. Fold the leaves like a roll, and put in an ovenproof dish with the folded sides up. Pour boiling cabbage water over the stuffed leaves and put in oven, preheated to 375 °F, for about 20 minutes.

Cook remaining chestnuts in melted butter and honey until golden.

The remaining cabbage water may be thickened and used as a sauce.

If you use fresh chestnuts, you need 1 pound. They must be cooked as described in the following recipe.

KOHLRABI POT

1 pound leeks
Oil
1½ pounds kohlrabi
1 teaspoon allspice
1 vegetable bouillon cube
1 cup water
1¼ cups sour cream
½ pound mushrooms
1 bunch parsley

Sauté sliced leeks in oil. Peel kohlrabi and cut into finger-thick sticks. Add kohlrabi sticks to leeks, together with ground allspice, bouillon cube, and 1 cup water. Let vegetables simmer over low heat for about 25 minutes. Add sour cream and heat. Add salt to taste.

Fry sliced mushrooms in oil. Spoon over vegetables and serve sprinkled with chopped parsley.

Instead of using sour cream, you can use a little more water and thicken with flour.

STUFFED ONIONS I

8 large onions
4 tomatoes
¼ cup peanuts, shelled
1 egg
½ cup wheat germ
2 tablespoons fresh, chopped basil
1 cup milk
½ cup tomato juice

Boil onions for 15 minutes. Hollow out ¾ of each onion. Finely chop the onion removed.

Dip tomatoes in boiling water for 30 seconds, then in cold water for 60 seconds. Peel and chop. Mix them with about ½ of the chopped onions, plus the chopped peanuts, beaten egg, wheat germ, and 1 tablespoon chopped basil. Add salt to taste.

Mix the second tablespoon of basil and the rest of the onions with milk and add tomato juice. Pour sauce into a pan that will permit the hollowed onions to stand upright.

Fill onions. Put in pan and let simmer, covered, over low heat for about 20 minutes.

Bake stuffed onions for about 20 minutes in oven preheated to 390 °F.

This dish is delicious with pâté or rissoles. You can also serve it with rice.

LENTIL CASSEROLE

1 cup lentils
1 vegetable bouillon cube
1 pound spring onions
4 tablespoons oil
½ pound mushrooms
1 tablespoon fresh, chopped lovage
Kuzo or cornstarch

Rinse lentils and cook for 30 minutes in a pint of boiling water to which has been added a bouillon cube.

Cut onions in quarters. Chop green tops. Sauté both in oil. Slice mushrooms and add to onions. Let simmer for 8 minutes, then mix with lentils and chopped lovage.

Heat the casserole, and, if necessary, thicken it with a little kuzo or cornstarch mixed with a little water. Salt may be added to taste.

Serve cooked rice or baked vegetables with this dish.

Lasagne

Lasagne is an Italian dish consisting of wide pasta bands put in layers with either a vegetable or meat sauce in between, then baked with cheese.

GREEN LASAGNE

1 pound broccoli
1 onion
Oil
½ pound mushrooms
2 cloves garlic
1½ teaspoons crushed rosemary
1½ teaspoons crushed marjoram
½ pound peas
2 tablespoons butter
4 tablespoons flour
2 cups vegetable water and milk
Nutmeg
1 bunch parsley
20 small green lasagne noodles, or 10 large ones
5 ounces mozzarella cheese

Separate broccoli into florets, dice stalks. Cook broccoli in boiling water for 7 minutes. Drain, and save water for sauce.

Chop onion and sauté in oil. Add sliced mushrooms and minced garlic.

Sprinkle crushed herbs on top and let vegetables simmer for 5 minutes. Then add broccoli and fresh raw peas.

To make a sauce, melt butter, add flour and make a roux, then add hot liquid, and stir until smooth. Add ground nutmeg, and if wanted, salt and pepper to taste. Chop parsley and add to sauce.

Grease an ovenproof dish. Put 1 layer of lasagne (check box to see if it needs cooking first), then a layer of vegetables, then sauce. Continue this process until all ingredients have been used. The top layer should be sauce. Top with sliced cheese.

If lasagne has not been cooked first, it must be completely covered by the sauce, otherwise it will remain hard.

Put dish in oven, preheated to 435 °F, for about 30 minutes.

You can serve a tomato salad or a mixed salad with this dish.

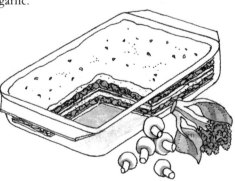

KALE LASAGNE

1 cup whole wheat grains
1 pound kale
1 onion
Oil
½ pound mushrooms
1 cup cottage cheese
¼ cup sesame seeds
4 ounces cheddar cheese

Rinse wheat grains and soak overnight. Cook in the same water for about 50 minutes.

Put whole kale leaves in boiling water and cook for 4–5 minutes. The coarse veins of the leaves must be tender.

Sauté chopped onion in oil. Add sliced mushrooms and let simmer for 5 minutes.

Drain water from wheat grains and save for later use for a soup or sauce. Mix drained wheat grains with cottage cheese together with crushed herbs and sesame seeds. Add salt to taste.

Put a layer of kale in a greased, ovenproof dish, then add a layer of wheat/cottage cheese and a layer of onion/mushrooms. Continue this process until all ingredients have been used. The top layer should be the cottage cheese and wheat. Slice cheese and put on top. Bake this dish in the oven, preheated to 375 °F, for about 30 minutes, or until cheese is golden.

EARLY GARDEN TURNIP PIE

½ cup farmer's cheese or cottage cheese
7 tablespoons butter
½ cup whole wheat flour
1¼ cups all-purpose flour
2 small early garden turnips
4 tomatoes
1¼ cups farmer's cheese
1 egg
1 teaspoon crushed rosemary
1 teaspoon crushed marjoram
½ cup stuffed olives

Briefly knead together ½ cup farmer's cheese, butter, and whole wheat flour with as much all-purpose flour as the dough will take. Put dough in a bowl and set in a cool place for 30 minutes.

Roll out ¾ of the dough and put it in a greased pie pan. Press dough up along sides of plate. Bake pie shell for 15 minutes in a 390 °F oven.

Thinly slice early garden turnips.

Cook them for 5 minutes and drain. Dip tomatoes in boiling water for 30 seconds, in cold water for 60 seconds, then peel and slice.

Mix the 1¼ cups farmer's cheese with most of the beaten egg (save some for brushing top of pie). Add rosemary, marjoram, and salt if desired, to farmer's cheese. Spoon this mixture into the baked piecrust. Top with turnip slices and tomatoes, and cover with sliced olives.

Roll out the rest of the dough and put on as a top crust, pressing the edges firmly together.

Prick little holes in the crust with a fork and brush with beaten egg. Return pie to oven and bake until crust is a light brown, about 30 minutes.

Serve with a salad of sliced peppers, cucumbers, and lettuce, with a garlic dressing.

PARSNIPS WITH GREEN VEGETABLE/WALNUT STUFFING

2 pounds parsnips
1 cup bulgur
2 tablespoons oil
2 cups water
½ cup milk
4 tablespoons chopped chervil
1 bunch parsley
⅓ cup chopped walnuts

Scrub parsnips and cook in boiling water until done, 20–30 minutes, depending on size of parsnips.

Toast bulgur in oil; add water and cook for 15 minutes or until all the water has evaporated. Mix in the milk. Let stand for 15 minutes. Add chopped chervil and walnuts. Add salt to taste.

Toast bulgur in oil; add water and cook for 15 minutes or until all the water has evaporated. Mix in the milk. Let stand for 15 minutes. Add chopped chervil, chopped parsley, and walnuts. Add salt to taste.

Slice parsnips lengthwise. Put half of the slices in a greased ovenproof dish. Put walnut stuffing on parsnip slices. Top with remaining parsnip slices.

Heat dish in 390°F oven for 10–15 minutes.

Serve a bean salad or potatoes with this dish.

STUFFED PEPPERS WITH WALNUT SAUCE

4–5 large green peppers
1 onion
2 leeks
Oil
2 cups mushrooms, chopped
1 teaspoon crushed rosemary
1 teaspoon crushed thyme
¾ cup cream
2 cups grated cheddar cheese
1 clove garlic, minced
1 bunch parsley, chopped
⅓ cup walnuts, chopped

Prepare peppers as described in next recipe.

Sauté chopped onion and sliced leeks in oil, until leeks are almost done. Add chopped mushrooms, rosemary, and thyme. Let vegetables simmer for a couple of minutes more.

Heat cream. Add grated cheese and stir until cheese is melted. Do not let sauce boil. Add minced garlic, chopped parsley, and walnut pieces.

Put pepper halves in a greased, ovenproof dish and fill with vegetable filling. Pour walnut sauce over peppers and bake in oven, preheated to 390°F, for about 20 minutes.

THE DOCTOR'S STUFFED PEPPERS

8 tablespoons cracked wheat or 1 cup
   cooked whole wheat cereal
4–5 large green peppers
2 onions
Oil
3 cups mushrooms, chopped
½ cauliflower head
½ tablespoon fresh, chopped basil
½ tablespoon fresh, chopped oregano
1 vegetable bouillon cube
6 tablespoons boiling water
¾ pound farmer's cheese
1¼ cups milk or cream
Kuzo or cornstarch

Soak cracked wheat for 8 hours, then boil for 30 minutes.

Boil whole peppers for 2 minutes. Halve lengthwise and remove seeds and membranes.

Sauté chopped onions in oil. Add chopped mushrooms. Separate cauliflower into small florets, dicing stalks. Mix cauliflower with onions, mushrooms, and herbs. Cover and let vegetables simmer over low heat for 5 minutes.

Dissolve bouillon cube in 6 tablespoons boiling water (from cracked wheat). Mix in the drained wheat, sautéed vegetables, and farmer's cheese. Add salt to taste, if desired.

Bring milk or cream to a boil and thicken with a small amount of kuzo or cornstarch mixed with water. Sauce may be flavored with finely chopped basil, and salt and pepper to taste.

Pour sauce in ovenproof dish. Put the pepper halves in the sauce and spoon filling into the pepper halves. Put dish in oven, preheated to 390 °F, for 20 minutes.

Serve a potato dish with these peppers.

STUFFED PEPPERS WITH TOMATO SAUCE

4–5 large yellow or red peppers
1 onion, chopped
Oil
2 cups mushrooms, chopped
1 pound tomatoes
½ cup corn
⅓ cup almonds, coarsely chopped
⅓ cup sunflower seeds
1 bunch parsley, chopped
1 onion
1 teaspoon crushed basil
1 teaspoon ground oregano
1 cup milk
¼ cup tomato purée

Prepare peppers and halve as described in "The Doctor's Stuffed Peppers" recipe.

Sauté the chopped onion and mushrooms in oil.

Dip tomatoes in boiling water for 30 seconds, then in cold water for 60 seconds, peel, and cut into small pieces. Mix a quarter of the tomatoes with onion, mushrooms, and corn. Simmer for a couple of minutes. Remove pan from heat and add coarsely chopped almonds, sunflower seeds, and chopped parsley.

Chop the second onion and sauté in oil. Add the rest of the tomatoes together with herbs and milk. Cook sauce until it becomes thick, then add tomato purée. If desired, add salt and honey to taste.

Pour sauce into ovenproof dish. Put pepper halves in the sauce and spoon filling into them. Put dish in oven, preheated to 390 °F, for 20 minutes.

Pour sauce in ovenproof dish. Put the pepper halves in the sauce and spoon filling into the pepper halves. Put dish in oven, preheated to 390 °F, for 20 minutes.

Serve cooked rice with this dish.

ITALIAN RISOTTO

3 onions
4 tablespoons oil
2 cloves garlic
2 cups brown rice
1½ teaspoons turmeric
½ tablespoon fresh, chopped basil
½ tablespoon fresh, chopped marjoram
4 cups boiling water
2½ cups mushrooms
1 green pepper
1 red pepper
1 cup peas
1 cup corn
½ cup black olives

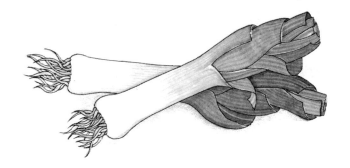

Sauté chopped onions in oil with pressed garlic. Add rice, turmeric, and herbs. Stir the rice in the oil for a couple of minutes. Add boiling water and a pinch of salt. Cook the rice for 40 minutes.

Slice the mushrooms and chop the peppers and add these, plus the peas and corn, to rice during the last 8 minutes of cooking. Add the black olives last so that they will be just warmed through.

Serve a green salad with this dish.

WHOLE GRAIN PANCAKES WITH LEEKS

½ cup whole grain wheat flour
½ cup all-purpose flour
2¼ cups milk
1 egg
3 tablespoons oil
6 thick or 12 thin leeks
½ portion of carrot purée (see page 143)
1–2 teaspoons crushed thyme

Beat the flour with the milk. Add egg and oil and let batter rest for about 15 minutes. Make 12 pancakes.

Cook leeks until tender and drain.

Spoon carrot purée on pancakes. Place a whole or half leek on top and sprinkle with thyme. Roll up pancakes.

Put the rolled pancakes in a greased, ovenproof dish and warm them in the oven, preheated to 390°F, for about 10 minutes.

SWEET AND SOUR BEETS

4 onions
¼ cup olive oil
1½ pounds beets
2 cups apple cider
6 tablespoons herbal vinegar
1 cup whole grain, presoaked wheat
⅓ cup raisins
2 teaspoons crushed thyme
3 tablespoons mango chutney
2 tablespoons honey

Sauté chopped onions in oil. Peel the beets, cut in cubes, and add to onions. Put apple cider, vinegar, wheat, raisins, thyme, mango chutney, and honey in a pan with the beets and onions.

Simmer covered for about 50 minutes. Watch that it does not dry out and burn. Before serving, you can add a little honey and a dash of salt to taste.

Sweet and sour beets go well with zucchini au gratin.

BEETS WITH YOGURT DRESSING

2 pounds beets
1½ cups yogurt
2 hardboiled eggs
1 bunch parsley
3 onions   .
Oil

Boil or bake the beets until tender, and peel. Let cool, then slice and put in a dish. Stir yogurt with chopped eggs and finely cut parsley. Add a dash of salt to taste. Pour this dressing over the beets.

Sauté sliced onions in oil. Cool and spoon over beets.

You can serve baked potatoes or whole wheat bread and a salad with this dish.

BAKED BABY BEETS

12 small beets
5 potatoes
3 tablespoons butter
1 egg (may be omitted)
½ cup milk
2 tablespoons tamari
1 tablespoon fresh, chopped marjoram
1 tablespoon fresh, chopped savory
½ cup millet flakes
10 stuffed olives
1 bunch parsley

Cook the beets until tender, and peel. Put them in a greased, ovenproof dish. If you are using large beets, slice them.

Peel potatoes, dice, and cook until tender. Drain and steam-dry over low heat. Mash potatoes and stir in butter, egg (may be omitted), milk, tamari, and herbs. Add salt and pepper to taste.

Spoon mashed potatoes over beets and sprinkle with millet flakes. Put dish in oven, preheated to 390°F, for 25 minutes.

Serve garnished with sliced olives and chopped parsley.

A green salad with cooked garbanzo beans and fresh cauliflower may be served with this dish.

BAKED BEETS I

1½ pounds beets
Oil
1 onion
½ head of cauliflower
1½ cups sour cream or crème fraîche
3 tablespoons fresh dill weed
¼ cup sesame seeds

Peel beets, slice less than ½ inch thick, and put all but 2 slices in a greased, shallow ovenproof dish. Brush with oil. Chop onion and sprinkle over beets. Put dish in oven, preheated to 390°F, for 35 minutes.

Separate cauliflower into small florets and finely chop the stalk. Grate the 2 slices of beet and stir into the cream with the cauliflower, dill, and sesame seeds. Salt can be added to taste.

Remove beets from oven and pour the cream mixture over them. Put back in oven and bake until beet slices are tender, about 20 minutes.

Wheat or lentil rissoles, or a green salad, are very tasty with this dish.

BEET SANDWICH CASSEROLE

2 pounds large round beets
1½ cups cottage cheese
1 large egg
4 tablespoons fresh, chopped celery
    leaves
1 tablespoon fresh, chopped marjoram
1 onion
Oil

Cook beets until done, peel, and slice. Drain any excess liquid from cottage cheese, then stir in the egg.

Sauté chopped celery, marjoram, and finely chopped onion in oil for a couple of minutes and stir into the cottage cheese.

Put half of the beet slices in a greased, ovenproof dish, then add the cottage cheese mixture. Lightly press the remaining beet slices on top of the cottage cheese mixture. If any is left over, spoon on top of the "sandwich."

Put dish in oven, preheated to 390 °F, for 25–30 minutes.

Rösti and a salad can be served with this dish.

CELERIAC WITH MUSHROOMS AU GRATIN

1 celeriac
2½ cups mushrooms
Oil
½ tablespoon lemon juice
1 onion
2 leeks
3 tablespoons flour
2 cups milk and celeriac water
Nutmeg
½ cup sesame seeds

Cut celeriac into 8 slices. Peel and cook until almost done. Arrange in a greased, ovenproof dish.

Slice mushrooms and sauté in oil. Add lemon juice.

Slice onion and leeks paper thin. Mix with mushrooms. Let vegetables simmer for 10 minutes. Add a little water, if needed. Sprinkle on a small amount of flour and thicken with milk or water in which celeriac was cooked. Reheat and add ground nutmeg, sesame seeds, and salt to taste.

Pour sauce over celeriac slices and bake in oven, preheated to 390 °F, for 20 minutes.

Serve with baked potato and a green salad.

CELERIAC A LA WIENERSCHNITZEL

1 large celeriac
1 egg (or soy flour thickening)
Granola or breadcrumbs
Oil
1 lemon, sliced
Capers
Horseradish
Butter
1 bunch parsley

Cut celeriac into 8 slices. Peel and boil for 4 minutes. Cool.

Beat egg. Coat cooled celeriac slices with beaten egg, and dip in granola. Fry slices in oil until golden.

Serve garnished with lemon slices, capers, and grated horseradish.

Melted parsley butter and boiled potatoes can be served with this dish.

QUEEN VICTORIA CELERIAC

4 small celeriacs (about 2 pounds total)
3 potatoes
2 onions
Oil
1 clove of garlic
1 cup mushrooms
2 teaspoons thyme
1 teaspoon coriander
½ cup grated Cheshire cheese
4 tablespoons cream
1 pound tomatoes
1 cup milk or cream

Peel celeriac and cook until almost done. Cook potatoes until almost done.

Sauté chopped onion in oil with pressed garlic. Add chopped mushrooms, crushed thyme, and coriander. Let simmer for a couple of minutes.

Grate potatoes and cheese and add onions and mushrooms. Stir in a little cream, adding salt to taste.

Cut "lid" off celeriac and hollow out. (The pulp removed may be used in either a soup or a salad.)

Put celeriac in a greased, ovenproof dish. Add filling and cover with "lid."

Dip tomatoes in boiling water for 30 seconds, in cold water for 60 seconds, then peel. Cut into small pieces and cook in either milk or cream. One tablespoon crushed thyme can be added.

Heat sauce; thicken with a little flour mixed with water, if necessary.

Pour sauce over celeriac and put dish in oven, preheated to 390 °F, for 20 minutes.

This dish is rather filling; you could serve it with a salad of bean or grain sprouts.

CELERIAC WITH RED NUT SAUCE

1 celeriac
1 onion
2 tablespoons butter
4 tablespoons flour
2 cups celeriac water and milk
½ beet
2 tablespoons fresh, chopped lovage
⅓ cup hazelnuts
Lemon juice

Slice and peel celeriac. (It is easier to peel it after it has been sliced.)

Put slices in boiling water and cook until done, 5-8 minutes. Keep warm.

Sauté chopped onion in melted butter until golden. Make a sauce by adding flour and the water in which the celeriac was cooked and milk.

Finely grate the beet and add it and the chopped lovage to the sauce. Add chopped hazelnuts, lemon juice, and a pinch of salt to taste.

Pour sauce over the warm celeriac slices in dish.

With this dish you can serve cooked brown rice with chopped pepper, glazed onions, and a green salad with a neutral dressing.

CELERY A LA ESPAGNOLE

1 large bunch celery
1¼ cups water
1 shallot
4 black peppercorns
1 bay leaf
3 tablespoons butter
3 tablespoons flour
1 bunch parsley
5 cups mushrooms
Oil
1 tablespoon lemon juice

Cut celery in 2-inch pieces. Chop leaves, if any. Put celery and leaves in boiling water with shallot, peppercorns, and bay leaf. Cook for 25 minutes. Remove onion, peppercorns, and bay leaf. Thicken with butter and flour. Add chopped parsley and salt and lemon juice to taste.

Sauté sliced mushrooms in oil. Add lemon juice and simmer for 5 minutes. Spoon mushrooms over celery.

Serve mashed potatoes or cooked whole wheat grains with this dish.

STUFFED SPRING CABBAGE

2 heads spring cabbage
2 tablespoons butter
Nutmeg
3 cups mushrooms
3 onions
Oil
½ cup cream
½ cup granola or breadcrumbs
2 eggs
Butter
1 bunch parsley

Quarter cabbage heads. Chop the coarsest part of cores. Put cabbage and chopped cores in boiling water and cook for 5 minutes. Drain and coarsely chop cabbage.

Melt butter in saucepan. Add a little ground nutmeg, and, if desired, salt. Sauté cabbage in melted butter until it is almost tender.

Sauté sliced mushrooms and chopped onions in oil. Let cool and mix with cream, granola, and beaten eggs. You can add salt and pepper to taste.

Put half of the cabbage in a greased, ovenproof dish. Add mushroom mixture and add the remainder of the cabbage. Put a few pats of butter on cabbage. Cover dish with foil and put in oven, preheated to 390 °F, for 30 minutes.

Serve sprinkled with chopped parsley. Boiled new potatoes and a dill sauce are excellent with this dish.

SPINACH PIZZA

1 cake compressed yeast
1¼ cups warm water
1 teaspoon salt
1 teaspoon honey
¼ cup oil
1½ cups whole wheat flour
2 cups all-purpose flour
1 pound spinach
½ cup milk or cream
1 clove garlic
Nutmeg
Cornstarch
1 cup stuffed olives
8 ounces mozzarella cheese

Crumble yeast in 85° water, letting sit for 8 minutes. Add salt, honey, oil, and whole wheat flour. Mix dough and knead thoroughly, adding as much all-purpose flour as dough will take. Let dough rise in a warm place for 1 hour.

Punch dough down and knead again. Roll dough out flat and divide into 4 small greased pizza pans or 1 large pan, or a cookie sheet.

Bake pizza crust in oven, preheated to 425 °F, for 8–10 minutes.

Cook spinach until tender with the water that clings to leaves after washing. Chop and put in saucepan. Add milk or cream and pressed garlic. Add ground nutmeg, and salt to taste. Thicken spinach with cornstarch mixed with water.

Spoon spinach filling into the 4 pizza crusts or 1 large crust. Top with sliced, stuffed olives. Garnish with sliced cheese.

Bake pizzas in oven, preheated to 390 °F, until cheese is golden, 20 minutes.

A tossed salad with the pizzas will make a delightful meal.

SPINACH/FETTUCINE CASSEROLE

¾ pound fettucine
2 onions
Oil
1 clove garlic
3 cups mushrooms
1 pound spinach
1¼ cups milk
2 teaspoons cornstarch
Nutmeg
½ pound Emmenthal cheese

Cook fettucine in boiling water for 12 minutes. Drain and put in greased, ovenproof dish.

Sauté chopped onion in oil. Add pressed garlic and sliced mushrooms. Let simmer for a couple of minutes; then add spinach and 1 cup water. Let simmer for a couple of minutes, then add milk and thicken with cornstarch dissolved in a little water.

Heat, add ground nutmeg and salt to taste. Pour spinach sauce over cooked fettucine. Top with sliced cheese.

Put dish in oven, preheated to 390 °F, until cheese is golden, 25 minutes.

Serve with small portions of Italian bean salad.

FLORENTINE SPINACH

1 onion
2 teaspoons oil
2 cups brown rice
4 cups water
1 clove garlic
1 pound spinach
1¼ cups sour cream or crème fraîche
Nutmeg
½ green pepper
¾ pound tomatoes
1 cup grated cheddar cheese

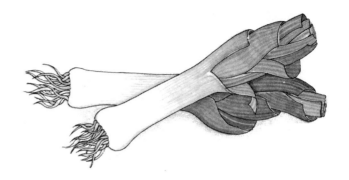

Sauté chopped onion in oil. Add rice, stirring it briefly in the oil. Add water and cook rice until done, 40 minutes.

Put rice in a greased ring mold, pressing it down. Sauté pressed garlic in a little oil. Add spinach and cook until tender in as much water as naturally clings to it after washing.

Coarsely chop spinach and return it to skillet. Pour in sour cream and heat. Add ground nutmeg and salt to taste.

Turn rice mold into an ovenproof dish. Pour spinach in center. Cut green pepper in rings, halve, and put on top of the rice. Dip tomatoes in boiling water for 30 seconds, in cold water for 60 seconds, peel, and quarter them. Place outside the rice ring.

Sprinkle grated cheese on top. Put dish in oven, preheated to 390 °F, and bake until cheese is golden, 20 minutes.

FRENCH ONION PIE

7 tablespoons butter
¾ cup buckwheat flour
¾ cup whole grain wheat flour
¼ cup sesame seeds
3 onions
3 leeks
2½ cups mushrooms
Oil
4 ounces Emmenthal cheese
2 eggs
1¼ cups sour cream or crème fraîche
Nutmeg

Cut butter into the 2 flours. Add sesame seeds and knead together briefly. Put in a cool place for 30 minutes.

Roll out dough and fit into a greased pie pan.

Bake in oven, preheated to 375 °F, for 10 minutes.

Sauté chopped onions, thinly sliced leeks, and sliced mushrooms in oil for 10 minutes. Spoon sautéed vegetables into baked pie crust with Emmenthal cheese, cut into small cubes.

Beat together eggs and cream. Add ground nutmeg and salt and pepper to taste.

Pour egg mixture over vegetables. Bake pie at 380 °F until golden, 25–30 minutes.

DANABLUE PIE

5½ tablespoons buckwheat flour
1 tablespoon soy flour
1 cup whole grain wheat flour
5 tablespoons butter
1 small egg
2–3 tablespoons cold water
All-purpose flour
5 ounces Danablue cheese
1 cup farmer's cheese
1 tablespoon cornstarch
1 cup sour cream or crème fraîche
⅓ cup coarsely chopped walnuts
Watercress

Mix the first 3 flours with butter, egg, and cold water using fingertips then add as much all-purpose flour as dough will take. Leave dough in a cool place for 30 minutes. Roll out and fit into a greased pie pan. Bake in oven, preheated to 390 °F, for 10 minutes.

Mix Danablue cheese with farmer's cheese, cornstarch, and sour cream until smooth. Add coarsely chopped walnuts.

Pour cheese mixture into baked pie crust and bake in oven at 390 °F until golden, 25 minutes.

Serve garnished generously with watercress. Serve half a portion of Celery a la Espagnole with the pie.

Zucchini

Zucchini is also called squash or courgette. It belongs to the pumpkin family and is native to the countries surrounding the Mediterranean.

Zucchini contains vitamins A (carotene) and C and very few calories.

SPINACH-FILLED ZUCCHINI

4 small zucchini
1 pound spinach
1 cup cream cheese
1 egg (optional)
Nutmeg
4 tablespoons chopped cashews

Boil whole zucchini until almost done, about 5 minutes. Then cut lengthwise and remove seeds. Steam spinach until tender in the water that clings to the leaves after washing. If you use frozen spinach, steam for a couple of minutes.

Remove pan from heat and stir cream cheese into the spinach. Let cool, then stir in the egg. Add ground nutmeg and salt to taste.

Put the zucchini in greased, ovenproof dish; spoon filling into hollows and sprinkle with coarsely chopped nuts. Bake in oven, preheated to 390 °F, for 15–20 minutes.

Serve a mixed potato salad with this dish.

ZUCCHINI WITH CHANTERELLES

4 small zucchini
1 fennel
1 onion
Oil
2½ cups chanterelles or other mushrooms
1¼ cups cream
Pepper
1 teaspoon crushed thyme

Boil whole zucchini for 5 minutes.

Remove fennel stalk, cook fennel for 15 minutes, then cut into cubes.

Sauté finely chopped onion in oil. Add chanterelles and let simmer for a few minutes, then add the cream. Cook over low heat until cream thickens. Add pepper and salt to sauce according to taste.

Slice zucchini lengthwise and sprinkle with thyme and fennel cubes. Pour creamed onion and chanterelle sauce over the zucchini. This dish may be heated in the oven.

A tomato salad and small new peeled potatoes, turned in melted butter, can be served with this dish.

ZUCCHINI WITH NUT FILLING

4 small zucchini
½ cup chopped cashew nuts
1 large red pepper
5 tablespoons cream
½ cup granola or breadcrumbs
2 tablespoons tahini
2 tablespoons crushed rosemary
2 onions
Oil
2½ cups mushrooms
2 teaspoons lemon juice
½ cup grated cheddar cheese

Cut zucchini lengthwise and remove seeds. Mix cashew nuts with very finely chopped pepper. Mix in cream, granola, tahini, and crushed rosemary. Add salt to taste. Spoon filling into zucchini halves.

Sauté onions, sliced into rings, in oil. Slice mushrooms and add onions and lemon juice. Let simmer for a couple of minutes. Put onions and mushrooms with pan juices in an ovenproof dish. Put stuffed zucchini in the dish and sprinkle with grated cheddar cheese.

Bake in oven, preheated to 375 °F, until cheese is golden, about 40 minutes.

Serve rice and a salad with this dish.

ZUCCHINI WITH WALNUT STUFFING

4 small zucchini
2 onions
Oil
1 clove garlic
3–4 celery stalks (with leaves)
½ cup chopped walnuts
2 tablespoons tahini
2 tablespoons chopped parsley
1 egg
½ cup grated Emmenthal cheese

Cut zucchini lengthwise, remove seeds, and arrange in a greased, ovenproof dish.

Sauté chopped onions in oil with pressed garlic. Finely chop celery stalks and leaves. If there are no leaves, use 2 tablespoons chopped, fresh lovage.

Add celery and leaves to onions. Cover skillet and let simmer for 5 minutes. Let cool, then mix in walnuts, tahini, and parsley. Stir in the egg. Salt can be added to taste.

Spoon filling into zucchini halves. Sprinkle with cheese and put dish in oven, preheated to 350 °F, until cheese is golden, about 40 minutes.

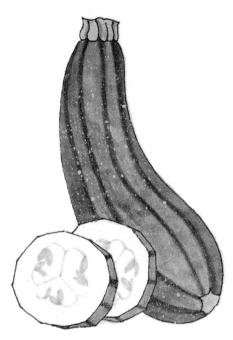

ZUCCHINI
STUFFED WITH HERBS

4 small zucchini
3 onions
Oil
2 ears corn
4 tomatoes
1 large egg
¼ cup granola or breadcrumbs
4 tablespoons chopped parsley
1½ tablespoons chopped fresh
  marjoram
1½ tablespoons chopped fresh oregano

Cut zucchini lengthwise, remove seeds, and arrange in a greased, ovenproof dish.

Sauté chopped onion in oil.

Put corn on the cob in boiling water (you can use frozen corn) and boil until done, 5–8 minutes. Scrape the kernels from the cobs and mix with sautéed onions and tomatoes, cut into little pieces.

Simmer vegetables for a couple of minutes. Let cool, then stir in egg, granola, and chopped herbs. Add salt to taste.

Spoon filling into zucchini halves. Put dish in oven, preheated to 375 °F, for 30–40 minutes.

Potatoes, whole grain French bread, or marinated beans go well with this dish.

A FRAGRANCE FROM THE EAST

The vegetarian can get much inspiration from oriental cooking. The basic principles of oriental cooking are that the fresh vegetables are chopped or finely cut, then stir-fried or steamed as lightly and as quickly as possible. This ensures the best possible preservation of taste, color, and nutritional value of the vegetables.

The oriental Yin-Yang philosophy is also found in cooking, where opposite poles are represented in combinations such as sweet/sour, spicy/bland, and soft/crisp.

Lightly stir-fried vegetables are frequently eaten in the East. The large Chinese frying pan—the wok—is an excellent utensil to have in the kitchen. It is a large, round frying pan, which allows the vegetables to be fried in portions, then pushed up along the sides away from the frying area as soon as they are done, but still crisp.

Brown rice is usually served with oriental food. The rice may be served either fried or mixed with vegetables. In India, the large flat bread, chappatis, or parathas, is often served with meals.

CHINESE VEGETABLES

4 carrots
3 leeks
1 early garden turnip
1 Chinese cabbage
1 green pepper
2½ cups mushrooms
2½ cups bean sprouts
2 cups peas
¼ cup corn or sunflower seed oil
1–2 teaspoons curry
1 teaspoon coriander

Finely slice carrots, leeks, and turnip. Chop Chinese cabbage, cut pepper in strips. Use mushrooms and sprouts whole. Heat oil in the wok or a large frying pan. Add herbs.

If you use a wok, cook vegetables in the oil for about 5 minutes. Push vegetables up along the sides as they are half cooked. When all vegetables are in the wok, it may be necessary to add a little water so that they can be steamed, covered, a little longer. It is important that the vegetables are not completely cooked. They should retain their crispness. Add salt to taste, if desired.

You can add to or subtract from the amount of vegetables used in this recipe. Fried rice goes well with it.

CHIENGMAI VEGETABLES

½ pound edible pea pods or string beans
1 head cauliflower
1 pound broccoli
4 tomatoes
2½ cups mushrooms
1 10-ounce can of baby corn, or equal amount cut from fresh corn on the cob
1 cup bean sprouts
¼ cup oil
2 cloves garlic
¼ cup tamari

Chiengmai is the largest city in northern Thailand. Crisp vegetables are served there, as they are everywhere in the East. Use the edible pea pods whole, but cut the string beans into small pieces. Separate cauliflower into florets and dice the stalk. Prepare broccoli in the same manner. Dip tomatoes into boiling water for 30 seconds, into cold water for 60 seconds, peel, and cut into small pieces. Use mushrooms, baby corn, and bean sprouts whole.

Heat oil and add pressed garlic. First stir-fry pea pods or beans, cauliflower, and broccoli for about 5 minutes, then add tomatoes, mushrooms, and baby corn. Add tamari, and let vegetables simmer covered for another 5–10 minutes. Add a little water, if necessary. Add bean sprouts at the last moment and heat them through.

Cooked or fried rice can be served with the vegetables.

CHINESE SWEET AND SOUR VEGETABLES

2 onions
4 leeks
1 celeriac
5 tablespoons oil
3 tablespoons honey
1 teaspoon ginger
½ teaspoon cayenne pepper
¼ cup garlic vinegar
¼ cup water
1 tablespoon miso
2 cups chopped Chinese cabbage
5 ounces rice noodles
⅓ cup almonds

Cut onions in rings, and leeks and celeriac in finger-thin pieces.

Sauté vegetables with honey, ginger, and cayenne pepper. Cover and simmer for 5 minutes, then add garlic vinegar, miso, and water.

Simmer vegetables for 10 minutes more, then add chopped cabbage and rice noodles. If liquid has evaporated, add water.

Stir vegetables in pan and let cook a few minutes longer, until noodles are done.

Blanch and halve almonds. Toast in dry pan and sprinkle on vegetables when ready to serve.

CHINESE SPRING ROLLS

1 cup whole wheat flour
⅓ cup soy flour
2¼ cups milk
¼ cup cream
3 tablespoons oil
1 egg (optional)
1 onion, chopped
¾ pound cabbage, chopped
1 carrot, grated
1 ounce rice noodles, broken into small pieces
Oil
1 cup bean sprouts
1 cup mushrooms
5 tablespoons tamari

Sift the two flours together. Beat in milk, cream, oil, and egg. Stir batter until smooth and let rest for at least 1 hour. Bake 16–18 pancakes, about 7 inches in diameter, on one side only.

Sauté chopped onion and cabbage, grated carrot, and noodles, and simmer covered for 5 minutes.

Cut bean sprouts into small pieces. Chop mushrooms. Add sprouts and mushrooms to vegetables in pan together with tamari. Let vegetables simmer for 3–5 minutes more, covered.

Put a couple of spoonfuls of the vegetable filling on the baked side of each pancake. Fold the edges and roll pancakes. Be careful not to break them.

Deep-fry rolls or fry them in oil in a frying pan. If fried in a frying pan, turn with 2 spatulas.

Cooked rice can be served with the spring rolls. If any filling is left over, mix it with the rice.

Spring rolls can be made ahead and put in the freezer. In this case, put filling inside rolls, and fry when ready to use.

CHINESE OMELETS ON RICE

2 cups brown rice
3 cups boiling water
4 eggs
8 tablespoons whipping cream
1 bunch parsley
1 onion
3½ tablespoons oil
1 cup finely cut cabbage
2 cups mushrooms
½ cup alfalfa sprouts or
   1 cup bean sprouts
2 tablespoons tamari

Toast rice in dry frying pan. Put in ovenproof dish and pour boiling water over it. Put dish in oven, preheated to 360°F, for 40 minutes. Stir rice once or twice. Add water, if necessary.

Beat eggs—one at a time—each with 2 tablespoons whipping cream and chopped parsley. Bake 4 thin omelets in a little oil.

Finely chop onion and sauté in oil. Add cut cabbage and mushrooms. Simmer vegetables for a couple of minutes; add sprouts and tamari.

Spoon vegetables on one side of the omelets and fold over.

When rice is cooked, place omelets on top. Return dish to oven until omelets are heated through.

Serve Sweet and Sour Chive Sauce with this dish.

BENGAL VEGETABLES

2 eggplants
1 Chinese radish
1 potato (if Chinese radish is not
   available, use total of 3 potatoes)
3 small zucchini
½ pound green beans
¼ cup corn oil
Fresh grated ginger
1 banana
Honey and natural mustard or Dijon
   mustard

Thinly slice eggplants, Chinese radish, potato, and zucchini. Cut beans into small pieces.

Heat oil in large pan and sauté vegetables for 5–10 minutes. Stir to prevent burning. Add ½ cup water. Cover and let simmer over low heat until they are done, about 20 minutes.

Add fresh, grated ginger to taste. Add a sliced banana and heat. Then add honey and natural mustard to taste.

Rice can be served with the Bengal Vegetables.

Chinese radish is a vegetable new to this country. It is long and red with a strong taste, similar to that of conventional radishes.

Sweet Potatoes

Sweet potatoes (yams) are not very well known in Europe. The sweet potato comes, as does the ordinary potato, from South America.

Sweet potatoes may be baked, boiled, or stewed. They are rich in vitamins A and C.

SWEET POTATOES IN SPICY SAUCE

2 small onions
5 tablespoons corn oil
1 clove garlic
1¾ pounds sweet potatoes
1 pound tomatoes
1 teaspoon ground ginger
4 cloves
2 bay leaves
1 pinch coriander
1 pinch cardamom
1 pinch chili powder
1 bunch parsley

Chop onions and sauté in oil with pressed garlic. Add peeled, diced potatoes. Let simmer a couple of minutes.

Dip tomatoes 30 seconds in boiling water, 60 seconds in cold water, peel, and cut into small pieces. Add to vegetables together with ground ginger, cloves, bay leaves, and herbs. Add water to almost cover the vegetables.

Cook vegetables until pan juices thicken, about 25 minutes. Salt can be added to taste.

Serve sprinkled with chopped parsley.

Cooked bulgur or rice with cut seaweed added, if desired, can be served as an accompaniment.

If you do not serve any accompaniments with this dish, you may add green beans or cooked lima beans to the sweet potatoes.

INDIAN CABBAGE ROLLS IN CURRY SAUCE

¾ cup brown rice
1 small head of cabbage
1–2 tablespoons curry
3 tablespoons oil
1 teaspoon coriander
1 small onion
2 cups mushrooms
1 cup bean sprouts
4 tablespoons almonds
⅓ cup raisins
½ cup sour cream or crème fraîche
2 tablespoons chopped parsley
2 tablespoons butter
1–2 teaspoons curry
3 tablespoons flour
1½–2 cups milk/cabbage water

Cook rice for 40 minutes.

Remove and discard outer leaves from cabbage. Put cabbage in boiling water. Carefully remove 16–18 cabbage leaves as they are cooked. Save cabbage water for the sauce. Chop the leftover cabbage and set aside. Sauté curry in oil. Add coriander and chopped onion.

Finely chop mushrooms. Cut bean sprouts in little pieces and add them together with a cup of finely chopped cabbage, to onions.

Let vegetables simmer for about 5 minutes.

Blanch almonds and coarsely chop them. Add vegetables together with raisins and cooked rice.

Let cool, then add cream and chopped parsley. Salt, and more curry, may be added to taste.

Put 1–2 teaspoons of filling on each cabbage leaf. Fold leaves around filling and roll. Set stuffed cabbage leaves with open end facing down in ovenproof dish. Pour in about ¾ cup cabbage water and put dish in oven, preheated to 390 °F, for 15 minutes.

Sauté curry in melted butter, stir in flour, and thicken with milk and cabbage water. Heat sauce well, adding salt and curry to taste.

Serve sauce and rolls separately. Serve cooked rice or boiled potatoes with this dish.

RICE
WITH BAKED BANANAS

2 cups brown rice
4 cups water
4–5 bananas
2 tablespoons butter
2 teaspoons curry
4 tablespoons flour
2 cups milk or vegetable bouillon
Mango chutney
⅓ cup almond slivers
½ cup black olives
1 bunch parsley

Boil water, add rice, and cook for about 40 minutes.

Put bananas in oven, preheated to 390 °F; bake until peel is black, about 10 minutes.

Sauté curry in melted butter. Thicken with flour and milk or bouillon to make a sauce. Taste for correct seasoning.

Toast slivered almonds in dry pan.

When rice is cooked, put it in a dish. Put peeled bananas on top and a tablespoon of mango chutney on each banana. Garnish with toasted almonds and black olives.

Sprinkle with chopped parsley.

Serve sauce separately.

INDIAN CURRIED CABBAGE

1 head of cabbage
3 tablespoons oil
1–2 teaspoons curry
1 onion
1 quart cabbage water/milk
Kuzo
1 teaspoon crushed coriander
8 slices pineapple
⅓ cup raisins
⅓ cup almond slivers
3 tablespoons butter

Remove tough outer leaves of cabbage before placing cabbage in boiling water. Carefully remove 10–12 cabbage leaves as they are cooked. Cook the rest of the cabbage until done. Drain, remove core, and chop cabbage.

Sauté curry and chopped onion in oil. Add cabbage water/milk and bring to a boil. Thicken with kuzo mixed with water. Heat sauce and add crushed coriander, and salt to taste. Add chopped cabbage.

Put a layer of cabbage leaves in a greased ovenproof dish. Spread a layer of the stew, half of the pineapple slices, raisins, and almond slivers. Then add a second layer of cabbage leaves and the remaining ingredients.

Top with the rest of the cabbage leaves.

Put pats of butter on top and place dish in oven, preheated to 390 °F, for about 15 minutes.

Caraway-seeded potatoes can be served with this course.

JAVA POT

2 medium onions
Oil
2 teaspoons curry
2 cups brown rice
4 cups water
4 carrots
4 leeks
3–4 teaspoons tamari
1 cup peas

Sauté chopped onion in oil. Add curry, rice, and water. Cook rice for 40 minutes. When rice has cooked for 25 minutes, add sliced carrots, leeks, and tamari. If water has evaporated, add more. Add peas 5 minutes before end of cooking time. Add dash of salt.

You can serve halved, hardboiled eggs, Spiced Red Cabbage, or a salad with this dish.

INDIAN CASSEROLE WITH CURRIED BANANAS

4 tablespoons butter
2 cloves garlic
1 teaspoon ginger
1 teaspoon coriander
½ teaspoon chili powder
1 teaspoon turmeric
2 eggplants
2 onions
3 tablespoons flour
2 cups vegetable bouillon
1–2 tablespoons mango chutney
4 tablespoons shredded coconut
⅓ cup raisins
½ cup cream
3–4 bananas
4 tablespoons butter
1 teaspoon curry
1 cup yogurt
⅓ cup almonds

Sauté pressed garlic and herbs in melted butter. Add cubed eggplants and chopped onions.

Let simmer for 5 minutes. Make a gravy with flour and bouillon. Add mango chutney, coconut, and raisins. Cover and simmer over low heat for 30–40 minutes. Add the cream.

Use firm, not quite ripe bananas. Slice them lengthwise and across.

Sauté curry in melted butter. Add banana pieces and fry for a couple of minutes on each side. Add yogurt and heat through.

Blanch almonds, halve, and toast on dry pan. Sprinkle toasted almonds over dish when ready to serve. You can serve cooked rice with this.

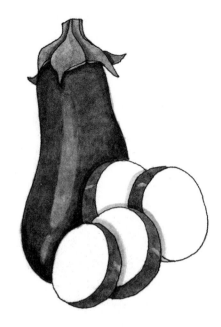

PÂTÉS & RISSOLES

Vegetable pâtés, rissoles, and cutlets are very tasty, economical, and easily prepared. They can be served with potato dishes and other dishes from the accompaniment section. Pâtés and rissoles are also fine for open-face sandwiches or for stuffing eggplants, zucchini, or peppers.

The vegetable fillings in these recipes may be frozen, thus making it possible to cook larger portions at a time. It is easier to bake or fry the vegetable stuffing before freezing, but pâtés can also be frozen in their uncooked state.

BEAN PÂTÉ

1 cup pinto beans
2 onions
3 carrots
1 ½ cups bean sprouts
Oil
1 bunch parsley
½ tablespoon fresh, chopped sage
1 tablespoon fresh, chopped marjoram
¼ cup sunflower seeds
¼ cup buckwheat flour
2 eggs

Rinse beans and soak overnight. Cook until tender in the same water for 50 minutes. Mash beans or put through a food processor.

Chop onions, grate carrots, and cut bean sprouts into small pieces. Sauté in oil for 10 minutes.

Stir vegetables into mashed beans. Add chopped parsley and herbs, chopped sunflower seeds, and buckwheat flour. Stir in eggs, one at a time. If mash is too thin, add more buckwheat flour. Add salt to taste.

Put pâté in greased ovenproof dish and bake in oven, preheated to 390 °F, for 40–50 minutes.

CARROT PÂTÉ

¾ cup brown rice
1 onion
6 carrots
1 large green pepper
Oil
½ cup chopped walnuts
1 bunch parsley
2 tablespoons soy flour
¼ cup whole wheat flour
1 tablespoon fresh, chopped basil
2 eggs

Cook rice for 40 minutes.

Chop onion, grate carrots, and chop green pepper very fine. Sauté vegetables in oil for about 15 minutes.

Add rice, walnut bits, chopped parsley, soy flour, whole wheat flour, and basil. Mix well, stir in eggs one at a time. If mash is too thin, add a little more flour. Add salt to taste. Put in greased dish and bake in oven, preheated to 390 °F, for 40–50 minutes.

MUSHROOM PÂTÉ

1 cup brown rice
3 cups mushrooms
1 onion
Oil
1 tablespoon lemon juice
1 carrot
1 beet
1 teaspoon crushed thyme
½ teaspoon crushed tarragon
½ cup cream
2 tablespoons soy flour
2 eggs
½ cup granola or breadcrumbs

Cook rice for 40 minutes.

Chop onions and mushrooms very fine and sauté in oil. Add lemon juice.

Add thinly sliced carrot and grated beet to the mushrooms. Let vegetables simmer over low heat for 5 minutes.

Mix rice into vegetables and stir in herbs, cream, soy flour, eggs, and granola to make a suitable consistency. Add salt to taste.

Put in greased dish and bake in oven, preheated to 390 °F, for 50 minutes.

LEEK PÂTÉ

6 leeks
1 onion
Oil
½ cup granola or breadcrumbs
¼ cup buckwheat flour
¼ cup chopped hazelnuts
2 eggs
1 cup cream
1 teaspoon crushed thyme

Slice leeks and onion fine. Sauté in oil until tender, about 15 minutes, on low heat.

Whisk together granola, buckwheat flour, nuts, eggs, cream, and thyme. Add vegetables when slightly cooked. Add salt to taste.

Put pâté in a greased mold; sprinkle with granola. Bake in oven, preheated to 360 °F, for 40–50 minutes.

GREEN PÂTÉ

1 pound kale
1 pound leeks
Corn oil
¾ cup brown rice
½ cup vegetable bouillon
1 bunch parsley
½ cup granola
½ cup whole wheat flour
2 eggs
1 teaspoon crushed marjoram
1 teaspoon crushed thyme

Boil kale for 8 minutes. Drain, remove coarsest threads, and chop kale coarsely. If frozen kale is used, cook it a couple of minutes until liquid has evaporated.

Cut leeks in thin slices and sauté in oil. Cover and let simmer for about 15 minutes.

Cook rice for 40 minutes. Mix kale, leeks, and rice with the bouillon. Add chopped parsley, granola, and flour. Stir in eggs, one at a time. Add crushed marjoram and thyme, and salt to taste.

Put pâté in oiled mold and bake in oven, preheated to 390 °F, for 40–50 minutes.

CELERIAC PÂTÉ

1 celeriac
2 potatoes
2 eggs
4 tablespoons fresh, chopped lovage
1 tablespoon fresh, chopped basil
1 cup granola
1 avocado
2 tablespoons lemon juice
Oil

Peel and cube celeriac and potatoes. Cook until done, drain, and force through strainer.

When purée has cooled, stir in eggs, herbs, and granola. Add salt and pepper to taste.

Peel and slice avocado. Coat avocado slices with lemon juice.

Put half of pâté in a greased rectangular baking pan or in a pâté mold. Put avocado slices on top. Add remaining pâté and bake in oven, preheated to 390 °F, until surface is golden, about 40 minutes.

MUNG BEAN PÂTÉ

(Serves 8)
1 cup mung beans
2 leeks
1½ cups mushrooms
Corn oil
1 clove garlic
1 tablespoon lemon juice
1 cup cream
2 egg yolks
3 eggs
½ cup buckwheat grits
½ cup granola
½ tablespoon fresh, chopped tarragon
12 stuffed olives

Rinse mung beans and soak for a couple of hours. Cook in the same water until done, about 30 minutes.

Slice leeks. Finely chop mushrooms and sauté both in oil with pressed garlic. Add lemon juice. Cover and simmer for 10 minutes.

Drain beans and purée in blender with the cream.

Purée vegetables in blender with egg yolks and whole eggs.

Combine bean and vegetable purée with buckwheat grits, granola, and tarragon. Add salt and pepper to taste.

Put pâté in a large, greased pâté mold, or 2 smaller ones. Line mold with oiled aluminum foil, if you want to take the pâté out of the mold after baking and serve it in slices.

Slice green olives and press them vertically well into the pâté. Bake pâté in oven, preheated to 360°F, for 40–50 minutes.

It might be a good idea to double the amount of this pâté, since it keeps well in the freezer.

If you want to freeze it, do not bake it first. When you want to use it, remove it from freezer, thaw it, and bake as described above.

This portion will serve as a main course for 6–8 people, and you could serve cold potato salad, whole wheat French bread, and a large bowl of salad with it.

Cold pâté is very well suited as sandwich spread.

SPICED LENTIL-NUT RISSOLES

¾ cup brown lentils
1 large onion
½ cup hazel or cashew nuts
1 teaspoon fresh, grated ginger
½ teaspoon cayenne pepper
1 tablespoon tamari
½ cup granola or breadcrumbs
3 tablespoons soy flour
1 egg
Oil for frying

Rinse lentils and cook until done, about 30 minutes. Mash in a food processor.

Grate onion, chop nuts, and stir both into lentils with ginger, cayenne pepper, tamari, granola, soy flour, and egg. If mash is too thin, use a little more granola. Add salt to taste.

Make 15 patties and fry in very hot oil until golden on both sides.

BAKED BEAN LOAF

1 cup red kidney beans
3 tomatoes
2 tablespoons cut chives
1 bunch parsley
1–2 cloves garlic
2 small eggs
¼ cup granola or breadcrumbs
Cream
1 small green pepper
2 cups mushrooms
Oil
2 sheets frozen filo dough

Soak beans overnight and cook in the same water for 50 minutes.

Purée in food processor.

Dip tomatoes in boiling water for 30 seconds, in cold water for 60 seconds, peel, and cut in small pieces. Stir into bean purée together with cut chives, chopped parsley, pressed garlic, and most of 2 beaten eggs (save a little for brushing on the dough). Stir in granola or breadcrumbs with a small amount of cream,—until purée reaches a suitable consistency. Add salt to taste.

Sauté pepper cut in paper thin strips and chopped mushrooms for 5 minutes.

Thaw filo dough and arrange into 1 large rectangular sheet.

Put half of pepper/mushroom mixture in the center of the filo. Cover with

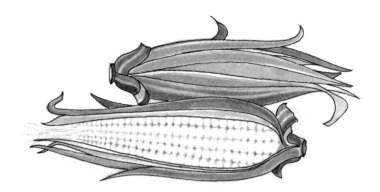

bean purée and top with remaining pepper/mushroom mixture. Fold dough around filling and place facing down in a greased ovenproof dish. Brush top with beaten egg.

Put bean loaf in oven, preheated to 420 °F, until dough is golden, about 20 minutes.

FRIED TOFU

12–16 slices dry tofu (fresh or canned)
Oil

Soak tofu in lots of water for 8 hours.

Drain the soaked tofu and fry on both sides in oil until golden.

Tofu may be served as a side dish, or used as a sandwich spread.

CORN CROQUETTES

1½ cups corn
¼ cup whole wheat flour
½ cup oats
½ cup granola (plus a little more for use as breadcrumbs)
½ tablespoon fresh, chopped tarragon
Oil

Purée corn in blender. If you use frozen corn, it must be cooked first. Canned corn may be used as is.

Stir mashed corn with whole wheat flour, oats, and as much granola as needed to give mash a suitable consistency. Stir in chopped tarragon. Add salt to taste.

Form about 12 croquettes. Dredge in granola and fry in very hot oil until golden on both sides.

WHEAT RISSOLE

1½ cups whole wheat
2 potatoes
1 onion
1 tablespoon fresh, chopped basil
1 egg
1 cup chopped almonds, other nuts, or
    sunflower seeds
¼ cup milk
2 tablespoons tamari
Oil for frying

Rinse wheat and soak overnight. Cook it in the same water for 1 hour.

Add peeled and diced potatoes to wheat after 30 minutes. After cooking, drain off excess water, if any, and purée wheat and potatoes in food processor.

Stir finely chopped onion, basil, egg, almonds, milk, and tamari in purée, which should be fairly firm. Salt and pepper may be added to taste.

Form about 13–14 patties and fry in very hot oil until golden on both sides.

MILLET CROQUETTES

1 large potato
1 quart water
1 cup millet
1 onion
⅓ cup shelled peanuts
Granola or breadcrumbs
1 tablespoon fresh, chopped sage
Oil for frying

Peel and dice potato. Boil potato cubes and millet for 30 minutes. Add more water, if needed.

Mash potatoes and millet and let cool. Finely chop onion and add to mash together with chopped peanuts. If mash is too thin, add a little granola. An egg also can be added.

Add sage, and salt to taste. Form 16–18 croquettes. Dredge in granola and fry on both sides in very hot oil until golden. Lower heat and fry 1–2 minutes more on each side.

This will serve 4 persons, but these millet croquettes are so tasty that you might want to make more than this recipe calls for. Any kind of croquettes may be used on open-face sandwiches.

LENTIL-RICE CUTLETS

1 large potato
½ cup lentils
¼ cup brown rice
1 pint water
1 onion
2 tablespoons tamari
1 tablespoon fresh, chopped basil
½ cup corn flour
1 large egg
Milk
Oil for frying

Peel and dice potato. Cook lentils, rice, and diced potato in water for about 40 minutes. If water evaporates, add more.

Drain off excess water, and mash lentils, rice, and potato together in food processor or food masher.

Stir finely chopped onion, tamari, basil, corn flour, and egg in mash. If mash is too stiff, add a little milk to obtain the right consistency.

Form about 10 cutlets and fry in very hot oil until golden on both sides.

FESTIVE GREEN FOODS

Most of the recipes in this book can be used in combinations and for festive occasions. The following recipes are for 5 different menus and a buffet serving eight persons.

These menus are designed for occasions that call for something extra.

STUFFED VINE LEAVES (GRAPE LEAVES)
·
STRIPED PÂTÉ
·
ALMOND LAYER CAKE

STUFFED VINE LEAVES (GREEK DOLMADES)

12 large vine leaves, or 2–3 times as
  many small vine leaves
½ cup brown rice
1 cup water
1 onion
Oil
¾ cup chanterelles or other mushrooms
2 tablespoons tomato paste
3 tablespoons sour cream or crème
  fraîche
1 tablespoon chopped parsley
1 tablespoon dill weed
1 cup vegetable bouillon
1 lemon

Fresh vine leaves are preferred for this dish. If you can get a large amount of vine leaves during the season, freeze them for later use. In this case, cook leaves for 8 minutes, cool, and freeze in required portions.

Canned vine leaves are available in some delicatessens, but the canned leaves differ considerably from both fresh and frozen leaves.

Remove leaf stalks. Put leaves in boiling water and cook for 8 minutes. Drain.

Cook rice for 40 minutes.

Sauté finely chopped onion in oil. Add finely chopped mushrooms and let simmer for 5 minutes, then stir in the rice, tomato paste, sour cream, and herbs. Add salt and pepper to taste.

Put a tablespoon of filling on each leaf. Fold edges and roll. If the small vine leaves are used, put 2 or 3 overlapping each other, then fold and roll around the filling.

Put the stuffed vine leaves in an oven-proof dish with the open sides down. Add boiling vegetable bouillon. Slice lemon thin and put on top of rolled vine leaves.

Put dish in oven, preheated to 390 °F, for 20 minutes.

Serve a lemon sauce with this dish.

STRIPED PÂTÉ

3 eggs
2 cups grated Emmenthal cheese
1 cup cream
Granola or breadcrumbs
1 pound carrots
1 teaspoon crushed thyme
¾ pound spinach
Oil
1 clove garlic
Ground nutmeg

Beat 1 egg. Stir in grated Emmenthal cheese and cream. Grease a rectangular baking dish and sprinkle with granola. Make sure that a generous amount of granola covers the bottom of the dish. Pour cheese mixture into dish and put it in oven, preheated to 360°F, for 15 minutes.

Cook carrots until almost done, then grate and mix with crushed thyme and 1 egg.

Spoon carrots on top of cheese and put dish in oven for an additional 15 minutes.

Cook spinach until tender in a small amount of oil and with pressed garlic. Add ground nutmeg to taste. Let cool, then stir in the last egg. Spinach should form the top layer. Put dish back in oven until spinach mixture has thickened, about 20 minutes.

Remove pâté from oven and allow it to cool for 5-10 minutes. Then turn it carefully onto a plate.

Serve baked potatoes and a salad with the pâté.

ALMOND LAYER CAKE

2 eggs, separated
3½ tablespoons unrefined sugar
4 tablespoons butter
2 medium boiled potatoes
2 tablespoons all-purpose flour
1 teaspoon baking powder
½ cup chopped almonds
Granola or breadcrumbs
½ cup fresh orange juice
1 teaspoon agar-agar
Honey
1 cup whipping cream
4 tangerines

Beat egg yolks with sugar until foamy. Add soft butter and mix to blend.

Finely grate potatoes and stir into the batter with flour, baking powder, and chopped almonds.

Whip egg whites until stiff and fold carefully into the batter. Put batter in 2 layer pans, which have been greased and sprinkled with granola or breadcrumbs, and bake in oven, preheated to 360°F, until golden, about 30 minutes.

Stir orange juice with agar-agar and heat slightly. Add honey to taste, if desired. Let set.

Whip cream until almost stiff. When orange jelly has set, whip it, and mix with the whipped cream.

Put half of orange cream on one of the cake layers. Separate tangerines into sections and put on top. Cover with second cake layer and top with remaining orange cream. Sprinkle slivered almonds on top.

FRENCH VEGETABLE PIE
·
NUTTY BEANS
·
CHERRY CAKE

FRENCH VEGETABLE PIE

1 pound frozen filo dough
1 pound broccoli or cauliflower
3 small potatoes
1 bunch chives
1 onion
2 tablespoons oil
1¼ cups cream
Kuzo or cornstarch
Nutmeg
½ cup black, pitted olives
1 egg

Thaw filo dough and separate. Put half in a greased pie pan (save the rest of the dough for a cover). Prick dough with a fork several times and bake in oven, preheated to 390 °F, for about 15 minutes.

Separate broccoli into small pieces. Dice stalks. Boil for 7 minutes. Drain well.

Cut potatoes into thin slices and boil for 5 minutes. Drain well.

Arrange potato slices on the baked dough. Add broccoli and sprinkle with finely cut chives.

Sauté chopped onion in oil. Add cream and bring to a boil. Stir kuzo or cornstarch with a little water and add to cream to thicken. Sauce should be rather thick. Add ground nutmeg, and salt and pepper to taste.

Pour sauce over vegetables and garnish with black olives. Top with second half of filo dough, pressing the edges of the dough together. Cut a cross on top to release steam.

Brush pie top with beaten egg and bake until surface is golden, 20–25 minutes.

You can serve one or several kinds of salad, such as bean sprout and tomato salad, with this pie.

NUTTY BEANS

1 pound French-style beans
2 ounces cheddar cheese
⅓ cup nuts
1 tablespoon fresh, chopped basil
4 tablespoons olive oil
2 tablespoons butter
4 lettuce leaves

Cut the ends of beans and cook for 5 minutes in boiling water. Drain.

Grate cheese and coarsely chop nuts. Stir cheese and nuts together with basil and oil. Add salt and pepper to taste.

Stir beans in melted butter until heated through. Arrange beans on lettuce leaves and spoon the nut paste on top just before serving.

CHERRY CAKE

½ pound canned cherries
½ cup cherry wine (or cherry juice)
⅓ cup raisins
9 tablespoons butter
3½ tablespoons unrefined sugar
3 eggs
1½ cups flour
1½ teaspoons baking powder
⅓ cup almonds
½ cup macaroons

Drain cherries and soak with raisins overnight in cherry wine. If you use juice, soak only raisins.

Beat sugar and butter well together; add eggs, one at a time. Add flour and baking powder. Beat batter, add 2 tablespoons wine or juice. Chop almonds and add half to batter.

Put half of the batter in a greased spring form. Crush macaroons and mix with 2 tablespoons wine or juice. Spread macaroon mixture on batter in form.

Sprinkle half of the remaining almonds on top of the macaroon mixture. Squeeze cherries and raisins and arrange on top. Spoon in remaining batter and top with remaining almonds.

Place cake at the bottom of oven, preheated to 390 °F, and bake for 40 minutes.

Serve cake either warm or cold with sour cream, whipped cream, or crème fraîche.

ST. LAURENTZ'S LEEK SOUP
·
ITALIAN BEAN CASSEROLE
·
FRUIT PARFAIT

The first course of this menu is a very old recipe which takes its name from a monastic order in Florence. Traditionally, the monks would eat this soup once a year on the holy St. Laurentz's Day.

ST. LAURENTZ'S LEEK SOUP

6 thin leeks
4 tablespoons oil
2 tablespoons all-purpose flour
2 cups vegetable bouillon
4 small slices white bread
¼ cup sunflower seeds
½ cup grated Parmesan cheese

Sauté finely cut leeks in oil, stirring until they are translucent but not browned. Mix well, and add hot vegetable bouillon. Stir in flour. Cook over low heat until leeks have boiled down to a mash, about 40 minutes.

Toast bread and place it in a soup tureen or in 4 individual soup bowls. Grind sunflower seeds and sprinkle on toast.

Pour soup over toast and garnish with grated cheese.

ITALIAN BEAN CASSEROLE

½ cup kidney beans
4 onions
2½ cups mushrooms
2 eggplants
4 tomatoes
1 clove garlic
Oil
2 cups milk
2 tablespoons butter
3 tablespoons flour
1 teaspoon crushed rosemary
1 teaspoon crushed marjoram
5 ounces Emmenthal cheese, sliced

Soak beans overnight and cook in the same water until done, about 45 minutes. Drain.

Quarter onions, cut mushrooms in half, slice eggplants and tomatoes. Sauté vegetables in oil with pressed garlic.

Bring milk to a boil and thicken with softened butter which has been mixed with the flour. Add salt to taste.

Put vegetables in alternate layers of beans, crushed herbs, cheese slices, and sauce in an ovenproof dish. The top layer should be sauce and cheese.

Bake in oven, preheated to 390 °F, until top is golden, about 20 minutes.

A green salad goes well with this dish.

FRUIT PARFAIT

⅓ cup nuts
2 peaches
2 slices pineapple
2 egg yolks
2 tablespoons unrefined sugar
1 egg white
1¼ cups whipping cream

Chop nuts and peel the peaches. Cut peaches and pineapple slices into small pieces.

Beat egg yolks and sugar vigorously. In a separate bowl, whip egg white and cream until stiff.

Put nuts and fruits in the beaten egg yolk. Fold whipped cream and egg white into fruit mixture.

Pour the cream in a mold and place in the freezer the day before it is to be used.

Thaw a little before serving.

GREEK EGGPLANT SALAD
·
BAKED PANCAKES WITH CHEESE
·
CARAMEL PEACHES

GREEK EGGPLANT SALAD

1 eggplant
1 green pepper
2 tomatoes
1 small shallot
1 clove garlic
2 tablespoons chopped pickled cucumber
1 bunch parsley
¼ cup sour cream or crème fraîche
4 lettuce leaves
8 black olives

Bake eggplant in oven, preheated to 360°F, until done, about 35 minutes. Peel and dice. Remove large seeds, if any.

Chop pepper finely. Dip tomatoes in boiling water for 30 seconds, in cold water for 60 seconds, then peel and cut into small pieces. Grate shallot and press garlic.

Mix all vegetables with chopped pickled cucumber and chopped parsley. Add sour cream and toss. Add salt and pepper to taste.

Place salad in a cool place until ready to serve.

Divide salad into four portions on lettuce leaves. Top with black olives. You can also use this salad as a filling for pita breads.

BAKED PANCAKES WITH CHEESE

1 cup whole wheat flour
2 eggs
2 tablespoons oil
1½ cups milk
2 tablespoons sesame seeds
½ teaspoon salt
Butter (for baking)
2 ripe avocados
¼ cup plus 2 tablespoons cream
1 teaspoon thyme
¾ pound green asparagus
1¾ cups milk/asparagus water
Cornstarch or kuzo
¾ cup grated Emmenthal cheese

Make a smooth batter of flour, eggs, oil, and milk. Add sesame seeds and salt, if desired. Rest batter for half an hour. Make about 12 thin pancakes.

Peel avocados and mash with a fork. Stir with cream until smooth. Add thyme, and salt to taste.

Put green asparagus in boiling water and cook for 8 minutes. Drain.

On each pancake put 1–2 tablespoons of the avocado and 2–3 tablespoons asparagus, then fold pancakes. Place them seam down in a greased ovenproof dish.

Bring milk and asparagus water to a boil and thicken with a small amount of cornstarch or kuzo mixed with water. Heat sauce and pour over pancakes.

Sprinkle cheese over sauce. Bake pancakes in oven, preheated to 390 °F, for 15 minutes.

Various salads can be served with these pancakes.

CARAMEL PEACHES

4 peaches
⅓ cup chopped nuts
¾ cup finely chopped figs
1 cup whipping cream
¼ cup plus 2 tablespoons unrefined
   sugar

Pour boiling water over peaches. Leave for 5 minutes, then peel. Place in an ovenproof dish and top with nuts and figs.

Whip cream until stiff and pour over peaches. Sprinkle with sugar and put the dish under the grill for a couple of minutes, or until sugar has melted and turned golden.

Serve immediately.

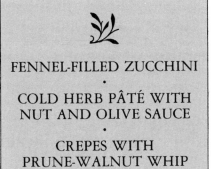

FENNEL-FILLED ZUCCHINI
·
COLD HERB PÂTÉ WITH
NUT AND OLIVE SAUCE
·
CREPES WITH
PRUNE-WALNUT WHIP

FENNEL-FILLED ZUCCHINI

2 zucchini (½ pound each)
Oil
1 fennel
4 tablespoons non-fat mayonnaise
8 tablespoons sour cream or crème
   fraîche
1 tablespoon fresh, chopped basil
¾ cup Emmenthal cheese, cubed
Watercress

Brush zucchini with oil and wrap in foil. Put in oven, preheated to 390 °F, and bake for 25 minutes. Cool, then cut lengthwise and remove seeds.

Cut stalk and green leaves off fennel. Save leaves. Cut fennel in half and cook for 10 minutes. Let cool, then dice.

Stir mayonnaise with sour cream and chopped basil. Add cheese, fennel, and fennel leaves. Add salt to taste, if desired.

Arrange zucchini halves in portions to be served, add filling. Sprinkle generously with watercress.

COLD HERB PÂTÉ

1 cup lentils
1 onion
⅓ cup hazelnuts
2 tablespoons sunflower seeds
2 tablespoons fresh, chopped basil
4 tablespoons fresh, chopped lovage
1 tablespoon fresh, chopped thyme
¾–1 cup whipping cream
3 eggs
1 large tomato
1 bunch parsley

Rinse lentils and cook until done, about 30 minutes. Mash them in food processor.

Grate onion. Chop nuts and sunflower seeds. Mix onion, nuts, sunflower seeds, and herbs with mashed lentils. Add cream, and stir in the eggs, one at a time. Add salt to taste, if desired.

Put pâté in oiled mold in the oven, preheated to 390°F, for 50–60 minutes.

Cool pâté. Serve garnished with tomato slices and chopped parsley.

Either bread or potatoes can be served with the pâté, in addition to:

NUT AND OLIVE SAUCE

1 pint milk or vegetable bouillon
½ cup black olives (pitted)
2 tablespoons chopped nuts
2 tablespoons butter
3 tablespoons flour
Lemon juice

Bring milk or bouillon to a boil together with chopped nuts and chopped olives. Mix butter and flour and add to sauce.

Heat sauce and add lemon juice, and salt to taste.

CREPES WITH PRUNE-WALNUT WHIP

6 tablespoons buckwheat flour
2 tablespoons all-purpose flour
1¼ cups milk
1 egg
3 tablespoons butter
5 ounces dried prunes
2 tablespoons honey
⅓ cup chopped walnuts

Beat the two kinds of flour with milk. Add egg and melted butter and stir. Let batter rest for 15 minutes. Bake about 8 small crepes.

Soak prunes for 4–6 hours in as much water as will completely cover them. Chop prunes and cook in the same water, together with honey and chopped walnuts, for about 15 minutes.

Spoon whip on pancakes. Either fold pancakes or roll around filling. Can be served either hot or cold.

BUFFET TABLE FOR 8 PERSONS

A "serve-yourself" table is an easy way to serve many. All the food can be prepared in advance. Cheese puffs, with the filling, and the almond pâté can be frozen.

The following serve-yourself table can be supplemented with other dishes and salads. And you can serve bread or rolls. For dessert, offer fresh fruit or cheese.

MUSHROOM PIE

½ cup whole wheat flour
6 tablespoons butter
¼ cup olive oil
¼ cup cream
5 tablespoons cold water
2 teaspoons crushed sage
½ cup all-purpose flour
2 onions
1 leek—or 4 spring onions
3 cups mushrooms
1¼ cups cream
1 teaspoon crushed oregano
1 vegetable bouillon cube
Cornstarch
1 bunch parsley

Mix whole wheat flour with butter, oil, cream, cold water, sage, and as much all-purpose flour as dough will take.

Roll out dough and put in a greased 12-inch pie pan. Prick with fork and bake for about 20 minutes in oven preheated to 360 °F.

Coarsely chop onions and cut leek into fine slices. You can substitute an extra onion for the leek. Sauté in oil until golden. Cut mushrooms in half and add.

Let vegetables simmer for a couple of minutes. Then add cream, oregano, and bouillon cube. Allow cream to boil down, using low heat for about 10 minutes. You may have to thicken with cornstarch.

Pour stew into pie crust and return pie to oven. Bake for another 10 minutes.

Serve garnished with chopped parsley.

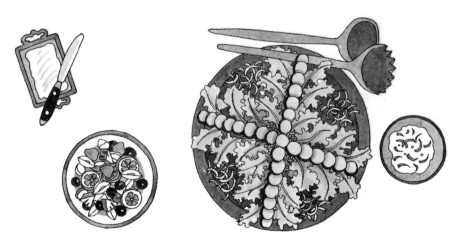

ITALIAN BEAN SALAD

½ cup lima beans
8 tablespoons olive oil
4 tablespoons herbal vinegar
1–2 cloves of garlic
3 tablespoons mixed, finely cut oregano,
  basil, and rosemary
Salt, pepper
1 shallot
4 stalks of celery
½ fennel
4 tomatoes
1 head iceberg lettuce
16 black olives

Rinse beans well and soak overnight. Cook until tender in the same water, about 1 hour.

Drain beans and let cool before the dressing is poured on.

Stir oil with vinegar, pressed garlic, and herbs. Add salt and pepper to taste.

Let beans stand in the dressing for at least 2 hours.

Finely chop shallot, cut celery in thin slices, chop celery leaves, cut fennel in strips, and cut tomatoes in wedges. Tear lettuce into small pieces.

Toss beans, vegetables, and black olives together in a large salad bowl.

POTATO SALAD

2 pounds small new potatoes
1 pound carrots
½ cup orange juice
Juice from ½ lemon
Salt
Pepper
1 bunch dill, chopped

Scrape potatoes and cook until done. Let cool. Scrape and thinly slice carrots.

Mix orange and lemon juices; add a small amount of honey, if desired.

Cut potatoes lengthwise and mix with carrot slices. Sprinkle with a pinch of salt and pepper. Pour on dressing and toss salad. Sprinkle with dill.

ALMOND PÂTÉ

½ cup cracked wheat
1 cup vegetable juice (or bouillon)
⅔ cup almonds
1 onion
2 stalks celery
1 tablespoon fresh, chopped marjoram
¼ cup whole wheat flour
2 eggs
½ cup granola or breadcrumbs
1 green pepper
3 ounces Emmenthal cheese, sliced

Pour boiling juice, or bouillon, over cracked wheat and let soak for at least 8 hours.

Grind almonds, chop onion, slice celery very thin, and chop the green celery leaves. Stir almonds, onions, and celery with the cracked wheat, marjoram, and whole wheat flour. Stir in the eggs, one at a time, then add enough granola or breadcrumbs to make the right consistency. It should not be too thick.

Cut pepper in strips and blanch a couple of minutes in boiling water.

Oil a pâté mold and sprinkle with granola or breadcrumbs. Put half of the almond mixture into the mold. Top with pepper strips and sliced Emmenthal cheese. Pour remainder of almond mixture in the mold.

Bake almond pâté in oven, preheated to 390 °F, for about 50 minutes.

CHEESE PUFFS
WITH AVOCADO CREAM

¾ cup water
5 tablespoons butter
½ cup plus 1 tablespoon flour
2 large eggs
½ cup grated cheddar cheese
2 avocados
2 tablespoons lemon juice
1 teaspoon thyme
1 cup cream
2 tablespoons chopped walnuts
12 slices cheddar cheese

Bring water and butter to a boil in saucepan. Remove from heat, stir in sifted flour, then return saucepan to heat. Stir until batter falls from spoon, and let cool.

Beat eggs and add to batter a little at a time, as much as batter will absorb. It should not be too thin, since it will run. Grate cheddar cheese and add to batter.

Form 12 puffs with spoon and place on an oiled baking sheet. Remember that puffs will rise to double size.

Bake the puffs at 390 °F for about 25 minutes. Avoid opening the oven door, since puffs fall easily.

If you want to freeze the puffs, let them cool, and seal in plastic bags.

When you want to serve the cheese puffs, cut off a "lid."

Halve avocados and remove meat. Mash avocado meat with lemon juice and stir until smooth, adding crushed thyme, cream, and chopped walnuts.

Put 1 or 2 tablespoons of avocado cream in each puff, cover with "lid" and top with a slice of cheese. Just before serving puffs, put them in oven, preheated to 390 °F, and bake until cheese is melted and golden.

SAUCES & ACCOMPANIMENTS

All main dishes may be supplemented with various kinds of accompaniments or side dishes. A potato dish is both a healthy and tasty accompaniment, and will go well with almost any main course. But there are many other possibilities, such as baked, au gratin, or stewed vegetables, as well as rice and pasta. Several of the first courses proposed in this book may also be used as accompaniments.

When choosing accompaniments, consider the final appearance of the meal to be created. A colorful accompaniment will enliven any dull looking main course.

Sauces are mainly used in connection with au gratin dishes. Therefore, this chapter includes only a small number of the lesser known sauces.

COOKED RICE

2 cups brown rice
2 tablespoons oil
4 cups water
Salt (optional)

Sauté rice in oil. Pour boiling water over it, adding a pinch of salt. Cook over low heat for about 40 minutes. Watch that it does not cook dry.

You may add chopped onion or pressed garlic to the rice.

If you wish to make a full course, you may add several kinds of chopped vegetables and herbs during the last 5–10 minutes of cooking.

BAKED RICE

2 cups brown rice
3 cups water
Salt (optional)

Toast rice in dry pan. Put in ovenproof dish and pour boiling water over it. Add a pinch of salt.

Put dish in oven, preheated to 360 °F, and bake for 40 minutes. Add a little more water during baking if necessary.

INDIAN PILAF

2 cups brown rice
3 cups water
¼ cup olive oil
¼ cup raisins
1 cinnamon stick
3 tablespoons almonds

Put rice in ovenproof dish. Add water, oil, raisins, and cinnamon, and put dish in oven, preheated to 360 °F, and cook until all liquid has been absorbed, about 50 minutes.

Stir coarsely chopped almonds into the rice when cooked.

PERSIAN RICE

1 shallot
4 tablespoons corn oil
1 clove garlic
1 teaspoon turmeric
3 tablespoons almonds
2 carrots
1 beet
3 tablespoons raisins
1¼ cups brown rice
2 cups water
¼ cup bean sprouts

Sauté finely chopped onion in oil. Add pressed garlic, turmeric, and slivered almonds. Let vegetables simmer for a couple of minutes.

Add diced carrots and beet together with raisins and rice. Stir a couple of minutes and put in ovenproof dish. Pour in boiling water.

Bake rice in oven, preheated to 360 °F, until all liquid has been absorbed, about 50 minutes. Add bean sprouts about 5 minutes before end of baking time.

FRIED RICE

3 cups water
1 teaspoon turmeric
5 tablespoons oil
1½ cups brown rice
2 onions
1 cup corn
½ cup chopped spinach

Bring water to a boil and add turmeric, 1 tablespoon oil and, if desired, a pinch of salt. Put rice in water and cook until all water has been absorbed, about 35 minutes.

Heat 4 tablespoons oil in skillet. Sauté chopped onion in oil. Add cooked rice together with corn and chopped spinach. Heat through.

COOKED MILLET

4¼ cups water
1¼ cups whole grain millet
Salt
1 bunch parsley

Bring water to a boil. Add millet and cook over low heat for about 25 minutes. Watch that it does not cook dry. During the last 5 minutes of cooking, you can add a pinch of salt and vegetables, such as peas or corn. When millet is done, mix in the chopped parsley.

WHOLE GRAINS: BARLEY, OATS, or RYE

2 cups whole grains
4 cups water

Rinse grains and soak for 12 hours. Cook until tender in the same water for about 1 hour.

You can add various chopped vegetables to the grains during the last 5–10 minutes of cooking. You can also cook the grains with rice or beans, in which case these should be added at the beginning of cooking time.

WHOLE BUCKWHEAT

2 cups whole buckwheat
2 tablespoons oil
3 cups water
Salt (optional)

Toast buckwheat in oil. Pour boiling water over and cook until water has been absorbed, about 20–25 minutes. Add salt to taste.

The buckwheat can be cooked with chopped or finely sliced leeks, or other vegetables may be added during the last 10–15 minutes of cooking time.

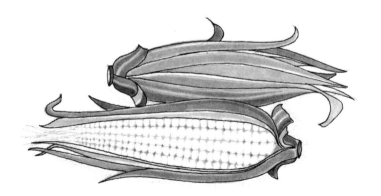

BAKED BEANS

½ cup azuki beans
6 tablespoons black-eyed peas
¼ cup olive oil
4 tablespoons honegar (half honey, half cider vinegar)
2 tablespoons fresh, chopped celery leaves
1 tablespoon fresh, chopped marjoram
1 tablespoon fresh, chopped oregano
½ pound scant frozen filo dough

Soak beans and peas for 8 hours and cook until almost done, about 45 minutes. Drain.

Stir olive oil, honegar, and chopped herbs together. Pour dressing over the warm beans and refrigerate for several hours.

Put beans in flat, ovenproof dish. Thaw filo dough, open, cover beans, and press firmly against sides of dish. Prick dough with fork. Brush dough with whipped egg or cream.

Put dish in oven, preheated to 390 °F, until surface is golden, about 30 minutes.

MACARONI TUBES

½ pound whole grain macaroni
1 cup water
1 tablespoon oil
1 onion
4 cloves
2 tablespoons butter
½ cup grated Parmesan cheese
½ cup grated Emmenthal cheese
½ cup milk or cream
Ground nutmeg

Put macaroni with oil, onion, and cloves in boiling water. Cook for 10 minutes. Drain.

Turn macaroni in melted butter. Add both grated cheeses and milk or cream. Heat through and add ground nutmeg, and salt, to taste.

BAKED MACARONI

½ pound whole grain or soy macaroni
3½ tablespoons butter
2½ tablespoons sunflower seeds
1 tablespoon fresh, chopped oregano
½ tablespoon fresh, chopped sage
1 green pepper
1½ cups grated cheddar cheese

Put macaroni in boiling water and cook for 10–15 minutes. Drain, and turn in melted butter.

Put macaroni in ovenproof dish. Sprinkle with chopped sunflower seeds and chopped herbs. Garnish with thin strips of green pepper.

Sprinkle with grated cheese.

Put dish in oven, preheated to 390 °F, until cheese is golden, about 20 minutes.

BAKED FETTUCINE

½ pound fettucine
1 onion
Oil
1½ cups mushrooms
1 green pepper
½ tablespoon fresh, chopped marjoram
½ tablespoon fresh, chopped basil
2 tablespoons butter
3 tablespoons flour
2 cups milk/vegetable bouillon
4 tablespoons chopped pumpkin seeds
1 cup grated cheddar cheese

Put fettucine in boiling water and cook for 10–12 minutes. Drain well and place in greased ovenproof dish.

Sauté chopped onion in oil. Add sliced mushrooms and simmer for a couple of minutes, then pour over fettucine. Add thinly sliced green pepper and sprinkle with chopped herbs.

Make sauce by melting butter, mixing in flour, and adding milk or bouillon. Heat sauce, adding salt to taste. Pour sauce over fettucine and sprinkle with pumpkin seeds and grated cheese.

Put dish in oven, preheated to 390 °F, and bake for 15–20 minutes.

The baked fettucine can be used as a main course for 4 if you increase all ingredients by 50 percent.

CHAPPATIS

1 cup whole wheat flour
About ⅓ cup water
Oil

Chappatis is a paper thin Indian bread.

Put flour in a bowl and make a hollow in the center. Add water, a little at a time, while kneading. Knead dough for at least 5 minutes, preferably longer. Cover dough with damp cloth and leave for 30–60 minutes.

Separate dough into 8 balls. With rolling pin roll each ball in a thin circle, about 4 inches in diameter.

Grease frying pan, preferably cast iron, and fry the chappatis. Press the dough into the frying pan with a damp cloth. Fry chappatis on both sides until crisp and brown speckled.

Chappatis will retain their crispness if cooled and kept in a cookie jar.

PARATHAS

These are stuffed pieces of bread, made from the same kind of dough as the chappatis. The stuffing can be various cooked vegetables, mixed in sour cream with curry, or sautéed mushrooms, placed on one half of the flattened dough. The other half is used to cover filling. The edges are pressed together with a fork and fried in the same manner as chappatis. However, you will find that you use a little more oil for frying, since parathas should not become crisp.

SAUTEED EGGPLANT WITH HERBS

2 eggplants
¼ cup oil
1 bunch parsley
1 tablespoon fresh, chopped basil
1 tablespoon fresh, chopped marjoram
½ tablespoon fresh, chopped sage

Dice eggplants.

Heat oil. Sauté eggplants with the herbs. Cover skillet and simmer over low heat until cooked.

FRIED PUMPKIN

1¾ pounds pumpkin
½ cup soy flour
Granola or breadcrumbs
Oil

Peel pumpkin and remove seeds. Cut pumpkin in finger-thin pieces.

Make a batter with soy flour and water. Dip pumpkin pieces in batter, then in granola.

Fry pumpkin pieces until golden in hot oil.

CAULIFLOWER WITH AVOCADO CREAM

1 head cauliflower
4 tablespoons olive oil
2 tablespoons wine vinegar
1 tablespoon crushed basil
1 large ripe avocado
¼ cup cream or milk
¼ cup chopped hazelnuts
1 bunch radishes, coarsely chopped

Cook cauliflower until almost done, then drain.

Make a dressing from oil, vinegar, and crushed basil. Pour dressing over cauliflower.

Halve avocado and remove meat with a spoon. Mash meat and stir in cream until smooth.

Add chopped nuts to avocado cream, then spoon over cauliflower.

Garnish with coarsely chopped radishes.

Serve either hot or cold.

CAULIFLOWER WITH OLIVE SAUCE

1 head of cauliflower
3 tablespoons butter
4 tablespoons flour
2½ cups cauliflower water/milk
½ cup chopped stuffed olives
2 hardboiled eggs
2 tomatoes

Cook cauliflower until almost done. Keep it warm.

Melt butter, add flour, and mix well, then add hot cauliflower water and milk. Stir and cook until thick.

Add the chopped stuffed olives. Add salt and pepper to taste.

Drain cauliflower well and place in a dish. Pour the sauce over it and garnish with quartered hardboiled eggs and tomatoes.

STEWED CAULIFLOWER

1 head cauliflower
2 cups milk
3 tablespoons raisins
½ teaspoon cardamom
3 tablespoons almonds
4 tablespoons chopped pumpkin seeds

Separate cauliflower into florets. Dice stalk.

Bring milk to a boil and add cauliflower, raisins, and cardamom. Cook over low heat for 10–15 minutes, or until it thickens.

Blanch and slice almonds. Add almond slivers to cauliflower. Sprinkle with chopped pumpkin seeds.

This dish has a sweet taste and is well suited as an accompaniment to spicy oriental meals.

BAKED FENNEL

2 fennels
¼ cup olive oil
1–2 cloves garlic
1 medium onion
¾ pound tomatoes
½ cup tomato paste
½ cup granola or breadcrumbs
½ cup grated Parmesan cheese

Cut stalks off fennels and slice the fennels. Chop fennel leaves, if any. Sauté fennel slices in oil with pressed garlic and chopped onion.

Dip tomatoes in boiling water for 30 seconds, cold water for 60 seconds, peel, and cut into small pieces. Put in frying pan together with the tomato paste. Cover and simmer for about 10 minutes. Add salt and unrefined sugar to taste.

Put vegetables in a flat, ovenproof dish. Mix granola with cheese and sprinkle mixture on top. Put dish in oven, preheated to 425 °F, for about 15 minutes.

NETTLE RING

5 ounces nettle sprouts
1 large onion
1 clove garlic
1¼ cups milk or cream
2 eggs
½ cup granola or breadcrumbs

Finely chop nettle sprouts and onion. Mix with pressed garlic. Stir in milk or cream. Add eggs and stir mixture with as much granola is it will take for a good consistency.

Grease mold, sprinkle with granola or breadcrumbs, then pour in mixture. Bake in oven, preheated to 355 °F, for about 45 minutes.

The ring can be filled with stewed carrots, and you can serve cooked rice or baked potatoes with it. Horseradish sauce goes well with the nettle ring.

CREAMED CARROTS

1 pound carrots
1 large onion
4 tablespoons oil
¾ cup vegetable bouillon
1 teaspoon honey
½ teaspoon crushed rosemary
1¼ cups sour cream or crème fraîche
1 bunch parsley

Cut carrots lengthwise, then 2 or 3 times across. Chop onion. Sauté carrots and onion in oil for 5 minutes. Add the bouillon, honey, and rosemary and simmer covered for 15 minutes. Watch that the water does not evaporate completely.

Add sour cream and chopped parsley and heat again.

CARROT PURÉE

1 pound carrots
1 parsley root
2 potatoes
2 tablespoons butter
5 tablespoons milk
1 bunch parsley

Dice carrots, parsley root, and potatoes and cook in unsalted water until done. Drain and let steam until dry.

Purée vegetables in strainer or potato masher. Pour purée into pan, heat, and beat in butter and milk. Add salt and pepper to taste. Serve sprinkled with chopped parsley.

You can make the purée with other vegetables such as cauliflower or Brussels sprouts.

STUFFED CARROT PIE

1 pound carrots
Oil
1 cup milk
2 eggs
1 bunch parsley
1 onion
1 green pepper
½ tablespoon chopped tarragon
1½ cups grated Mozzarella cheese

Grate carrots and cook in oil for 10 minutes. Let cool. Beat milk and eggs together. Chop parsley and add it and milk mixture to carrots.

Cut onions in rings and finely chop green pepper. Sauté both in oil. Add chopped tarragon and let simmer covered for 5 minutes.

Put half of the carrot mixture in a greased pie pan. Spoon in sautéed onion and pepper. Put Mozzarella cheese on top and add the remaining carrot mixture.

Bake carrot pie in oven (375 °F) for about 40 minutes.

BRAISED CARROTS WITH APPLES

1 pound carrots
3 tablespoons butter
¼ cup water
2–3 apples
2 tablespoons honey
1 bunch parsley

Quarter carrots by cutting lengthwise, then across.

Melt butter, add water, and simmer carrots for about 10 minutes.

Peel apples and cut in wedges. Add to carrots together with honey. Let carrots and apples simmer 10 minutes longer, or until carrots are done.

Serve sprinkled with chopped parsley.

BAKED CARROTS

1 pound carrots
2 tablespoons butter
3 tablespoons honey
2 tablespoons fresh, chopped lemon balm
1 cup milk

Sauté sliced carrots in melted butter and honey.

Add lemon balm.

Put carrots in ovenproof dish and pour milk over them. Bake in oven, preheated to 390 °F, until carrots are done, about 20 minutes.

FRIED JERUSALEM ARTICHOKES

1½ pounds Jerusalem artichokes
2 onions
¼ cup oil
1 clove garlic
1–2 teaspoons crushed thyme
1 bunch parsley

Scrub artichokes clean, then slice them. Chop onions and sauté both in oil with pressed garlic, thyme, and chopped parsley. Cover pan and let vegetables simmer over low heat until done. Stir occasionally. Add a pinch of salt before serving, if desired.

POTATOES AU GRATIN

½ pound French-style beans
1 pound potatoes, sliced thin
Nutmeg
1 cup sour cream or crème fraîche
3½ ounces cream cheese

Boil beans for 5 minutes. Drain and plunge into ice water. Cut into small pieces.

Layer potato slices and beans in greased, ovenproof dish. Sprinkle with ground nutmeg, adding salt and pepper, if desired.

Mix sour cream and cream cheese and spoon over potatoes.

Put dish in oven, preheated to 390 °F, for 45–50 minutes. If top turns dark, put a piece of foil over the dish.

CUMIN POTATOES

4 large baking potatoes
Oil
Salt
Caraway

Scrub potatoes and cut lengthwise. Brush with oil and put in an ovenproof dish. Sprinkle with salt and caraway according to taste. Bake potatoes in oven, preheated to 380 °F, for 40 minutes.

PARISIAN POTATOES

1½ pounds potatoes
3½ tablespoons butter
2 onions
1 bouquet garni

Cook potatoes until nearly done. Peel and slice.

Sauté chopped onions in melted butter until translucent.

Add bouquet garni and potato slices. Cover and cook potatoes over low heat until done. Add a small amount of water, if necessary.

POTATOES A LA PROVENCE

1½ pounds potatoes, sliced thin
½ cup olive oil
1 bunch parsley
1 clove garlic
2 spring onions
Nutmeg
Juice of ½ lemon

Slice potatoes.

Heat oil in large frying pan and add chopped parsley, pressed garlic, chopped onions, and a small amount of ground nutmeg. Stir in potato slices. Let simmer over low heat until done. Sprinkle with salt and pepper. Just before serving, add juice of ½ lemon.

BAKED POTATOES WITH PARSLEY ROOT

1½ pounds potatoes
1 parsley root
1 green pepper
¾ cup vegetable bouillon
¾ cup milk
1 bunch parsley
Paprika
2 onions
2 tablespoons oil

Thinly slice potatoes and parsley root. Cut green pepper into thin strips.

Blend bouillon and milk. Add chopped parsley, paprika, and salt to taste.

Pour this over vegetables and place dish in oven, preheated to 390 °F, for 50 minutes.

Cut onions into rings; sauté in oil. Place onion rings on top of vegetables when ready to serve.

POTATO CAKE

1½ pounds potatoes, grated coarse
½ cup millet flakes
1 onion
2 tablespoons oil
2 cups sliced mushrooms
½ cup milk
2 tablespoons butter

Grate potatoes and mix with millet flakes.

Chop onion and sauté in oil. Add sliced mushrooms. Simmer for 5 minutes, then mix with potatoes. Put in ovenproof dish. Pour in milk and add pats of butter.

Bake in oven, preheated to 390 °F, for 45 minutes.

SWISS RÖSTI

1½ pounds potatoes, grated coarse
4 tablespoons butter
½ cup Emmenthal cheese, grated

Grate potatoes. Melt butter in frying pan until golden, add potatoes and grated cheese.

Form a pancake (rösti) of the potato mix and fry over low heat for about 15 minutes, until golden; turn and fry on the other side. Add salt and pepper, if desired.

BAKED POTATOES WITH CHEESE

4 large baking potatoes
½ cup cream cheese
3 tablespoons walnuts, chopped

Scrub potatoes and bake in a 390 °F oven, for 50 minutes. Remove from oven, cut a lid off, and hollow out meat of each potato. Mash and stir cream cheese and chopped walnuts into potato removed.

Fill potato hollows and put back in the oven for about 10 minutes.

BAKED SESAME POTATOES

4 large baking potatoes
4 tablespoons milk or cream
4 tablespoons sesame seeds
2 tablespoons dill

Bake potatoes, hollow out, and mash potato as described in preceding recipe.

Stir in sesame seeds, milk, and dill, and add salt to taste. Fill in hollow potatoes and bake in 390 °F oven for 10 minutes.

BAKED OLIVE POTATOES

4 large baking potatoes
1 small shallot, chopped fine
8 stuffed olives, sliced
1 small egg (butter may be substituted)

Bake potatoes, hollow out, and mash as described in Baked Potatoes With Cheese.

Stir in shallot, olives, and egg (or butter). Put filling in hollow potatoes and bake in 390 °F oven for 10 minutes.

Baked potatoes can be filled with other stuffings. You could also cut a cross in the baked potato, press it open, and fill it with a pat of butter mixed with herbs, shredded horseradish, or pressed garlic.

BAKED SWEET POTATOES WITH PINEAPPLE

4 sweet potatoes
3 tablespoons almond slivers
½ pineapple
4 tablespoons corn oil

Slice potatoes lengthwise and put slices in greased ovenproof dish. Sprinkle with slivered almonds.

Chop pineapple and spoon over potato slices. Sprinkle with oil and bake in oven, preheated to 390 °F, for 40 minutes.

BAKED SWEET POTATOES WITH RAISINS

4 sweet potatoes
⅓ cup raisins
¾ cup water
½ cup wheat germ

Peel and dice potatoes and mix with raisins. Put in ovenproof dish and add water. Sprinkle with wheat germ and bake in oven, preheated to 390 °F, for 40 minutes.

BRAISED CHINESE CABBAGE

1 Chinese cabbage
1 onion
3 tablespoons butter
1 clove garlic
1 tablespoon fresh, chopped savory
1 bunch parsley, chopped
4 tablespoons chopped peanuts

Sauté cut cabbage and chopped onion in butter with pressed garlic. Stir cabbage for 8–10 minutes. Add chopped savory, parsley, and peanuts.

BRAISED KOHLRABI

1 pound kohlrabi, sliced thin
1 green pepper, chopped
1 onion, chopped
4 tablespoons oil
¾ cup vegetable bouillon
1 bunch parsley

Thinly slice kohlrabi, then cut into strips. Chop green pepper and onion.
    Heat oil and sauté vegetables. Add boiling bouillon and cover. Simmer over low heat for about 10 minutes.
    Serve sprinkled with chopped parsley.

STEWED SPRING ONIONS

1 pound small spring onions
1¼ cups vegetable bouillon
½ pound peas, shelled
1 cup milk
Kuzo
Nutmeg

Chop green onion tops. Put onions in boiling vegetable bouillon and cook until done, about 15 minutes. Add the chopped onion greens and peas 5 minutes before end of cooking time. Add milk and thicken with a little kuzo mixed with water. Add ground nutmeg, and salt to taste.

STUFFED ONIONS II

4 large onions
2 tablespoons oil
1 clove garlic
4 tablespoons chopped kale
2 tablespoons chopped raisins
2 tablespoons crushed granola or bread-
    crumbs
4 tablespoons milk
1 cup vegetable bouillon
4 tablespoons olive oil

Boil onions for 8–10 minutes, then peel. Cut a lid off onions and hollow out most of the onion. Chop this onion meat. One tablespoon will be used in this recipe; the rest can be used in a salad, a soup, or a sauce.
    Sauté 1 tablespoon chopped onion in oil together with pressed garlic, chopped kale, and raisins. Stir in granola or breadcrumbs and milk. Add salt and pepper to taste.
    Put filling in hollowed out onions. Pour vegetable bouillon in ovenproof dish. Add onions. Pour 1 tablespoon oil over each onion.
    Bake in oven, preheated to 375 °F, for 40 minutes.

GREEK ONIONS

½ pound small shallots
1 fennel
1 pound tomatoes
¼ cup olive oil
1 bunch parsley

Peel shallots, cut fennel in fine strips. Dip tomatoes in boiling water for 30 seconds, in cold water for 60 seconds, peel, and chop. Mix vegetables with olive oil and simmer covered for 30 minutes. Add salt and pepper to taste.

Greek Onions may be served either hot or cold, sprinkled with chopped parsley.

BAKED ONIONS

4 large onions
4 tablespoons oil

Peel onions and brush with oil. Put in oven, preheated to 390 °F, and bake until done, about 45 minutes.

GLAZED SHALLOTS

1 pound small shallots
¼ cup unrefined sugar or honey
2 tablespoons butter

Peel shallots. Melt sugar (or honey), then add butter. Put shallots in melted butter and let simmer over low heat until they are done, about 10 minutes.

BAKED PARSNIPS

4 parsnips
½ cup milk
¾ cup grated cheddar cheese
1 bunch parsley
¼ cup wheat germ

Slice parsnips lengthwise and cook until almost done. Put in a greased ovenproof dish.

Mix milk, grated cheese, and chopped parsley. Pour over parsnips. Sprinkle with wheat germ.

Put dish in oven, preheated to 435 °F, for about 15 minutes.

FRIED PARSNIPS

4 parsnips
1 egg (or soy flour and water)
Granola or breadcrumbs
Oil

Put parsnips in boiling water and cook until done, about 20 minutes.

Slice parsnips lengthwise and cool.

Dip cooled parsnip slices either in a beaten egg or in a batter, then in granola or breadcrumbs. Fry slices in oil until golden on both sides.

BRUSSELS SPROUTS IN ALMOND-RAISIN SAUCE

1 pound Brussels sprouts
2 cups Brussels sprouts water/milk
3 tablespoons cornstarch
3 tablespoons raisins
3 tablespoons coarsely chopped almonds

Boil Brussels sprouts for 7 minutes. Drain. Save water.

Bring 2 cups Brussels sprouts water and milk to a boil. Thicken with cornstarch mixed with a little water. Add raisins and cook for a couple of minutes.

Put Brussels sprouts in sauce and heat. Add coarsely chopped almonds.

STEWED BRUSSELS SPROUTS WITH NUTS

¾ pound Brussels sprouts
2 cups milk or water from Brussels
  sprouts
2 tablespoons butter
3 tablespoons flour
2 carrots, grated
⅓ cup chopped walnuts

Boil Brussels sprouts for 7 minutes, then drain.

Bring milk (or the cooking water from Brussels sprouts) to a boil. Stir softened butter with flour and use to thicken liquid to make a sauce. Add grated carrots.

Heat sauce for a couple of minutes. Put in Brussels sprouts and heat again. Add chopped walnuts. Season with salt and pepper to taste.

BAKED BRUSSELS SPROUTS WITH CHEESE

1 pound Brussels sprouts
1 cup milk or cream
1–2 teaspoons kuzo
1 bunch parsley
¾ cup Emmenthal cheese, grated

Boil Brussels sprouts for 7 minutes. Drain and put in ovenproof dish.

Bring milk (or cream) to a boil. Add kuzo mixed with water. Heat sauce. Add chopped parsley and salt and pepper to taste.

Pour sauce over Brussels sprouts. Sprinkle with grated cheese. Put dish in oven, preheated to 390 °F, until cheese is golden.

BRUSSELS SPROUTS IN TOMATO SAUCE

1 pound Brussels sprouts
1 pound tomatoes
¼ cup milk
1 clove garlic
Cornstarch or kuzo
1 bunch chives

Boil Brussels sprouts for 7 minutes. Dip tomatoes in boiling water for 30 seconds, in cold water for 60 seconds, peel, and cut in small pieces. Add milk and pressed garlic and boil, stirring constantly, until you get a smooth sauce. Thicken with a little cornstarch or kuzo mixed with water, if necessary.

Put Brussels sprouts in sauce and heat. Add unrefined sugar and salt to taste.

Serve sprinkled with finely chopped chives.

BEETS IN GARLIC SAUCE

1 pound beets
1 cup yogurt
1 clove garlic
4 tablespoons dill

Use either cooked or uncooked beets. If uncooked, peel and grate. If cooked, peel and either slice or dice.

Add pressed garlic and dill to yogurt. Add also salt to taste. Stir beets in sauce.

BAKED BEETS II

4 beets
Oil
1 cup yogurt
4 tablespoons chopped parsley
Grated horseradish

Brush beets with oil and put in oven, preheated to 390 °F. Bake until done, about 50 minutes.

Mix yogurt with chopped parsley, grated horseradish, and salt to taste.

Serve beets halved lengthwise and pour the sauce over them.

CELERIAC WALNUT CAKES

1 pound celeriac
¾ pound potatoes
1 cup grated cheddar cheese
⅓ cup chopped walnuts
1 egg
1 bunch parsley

Peel and dice celeriac and potatoes. Cook until done, drain, and steam-dry vegetables.

Mash vegetables, add grated cheese and walnuts, and mix with egg and chopped parsley. Add salt to taste.

Form 12-14 patties, using 2 spoons, and put on a greased baking sheet.

Bake in oven, preheated to 390 °F, for 30 minutes.

JERUSALEM ARTICHOKES WITH HERB BUTTER

2 pounds Jerusalem artichokes
Milk
4 tablespoons butter
2 tablespoons fresh, chopped basil

Scrub and peel roots. Put in cold water to prevent discoloring. Cut in pieces and cook until done, about 15 minutes, in equal amounts of milk and water, again to prevent discoloring. The milk and water can be thickened with cornstarch after cooking, and served as a sauce with the Jerusalem artichokes.

If you prefer to serve the Jerusalem artichokes with herb butter, melt the butter and stir in chopped basil. Pour herb butter over the artichokes before serving.

STEWED SPRING CABBAGE

1 large head of spring cabbage
2 tablespoons butter
4 tablespoons flour
2–2½ cups cabbage water/milk
Nutmeg

Cut spring cabbage into quarters, put in boiling water, and cook until almost done, about 8 minutes. Cut cabbage in strips.

Melt butter, mix in flour, and thicken with cabbage water and milk. Sauce should not be too thin. Add ground nutmeg and salt and pepper to taste.

Put cabbage in the sauce and heat. Sprinkle with chopped parsley or other herbs.

SPRING CABBAGE STEAMED IN BUTTER

1 large head of spring cabbage
4 tablespoons butter
Salt
Pepper

If you want to bring out the fine taste peculiar to spring cabbage, steam it in butter.

The cabbage can be cooked either whole, in quarters, or shredded.

Bring 1 cup water to a boil. Add butter, salt, and pepper. Add cabbage and cook until just done.

SPICED RED CABBAGE

½ small head of red cabbage
2 tablespoons butter
¾ cup red currant juice
4 cloves
1 stick cinnamon
½ teaspoon ground nutmeg
Honey

Chop cabbage fine.

Melt butter, add red currant juice, cloves, cinnamon, and ground nutmeg. Stir cabbage into this liquid, cover, and let simmer for 50 minutes.

Add honey, and salt to taste.

SWISS CHARD WITH MASHED POTATOES

8 stalks of Swiss chard
¾ pound potatoes
¼ cup milk
3 tablespoons butter
¼ cup sesame seeds
Nutmeg
¾ cup grated cheshire or cheddar
   cheese

Boil chard 8 minutes. Drain and put in greased, ovenproof dish.

Cook potatoes, peel, and mash. Stir in milk and half the butter. Add sesame seeds and ground nutmeg, and salt to taste.

Spoon mixture on chard leaves, then fold or roll them and put them in ovenproof dish.

Melt second half of butter and pour it over the chard rolls. Sprinkle with grated cheese.

Bake in oven, preheated to 390 °F, until cheese is golden, about 20 minutes.

Swiss chard leaves may also be filled with half a portion of vegetable filling or bean pâté.

USZKI (STUFFED BREAD)

½ compressed yeast cake
½ cup water
4 tablespoons corn oil
½ teaspoon honey
½ teaspoon salt
1 egg
1½ cups whole wheat flour
1 cup mushrooms
1 onion
Corn oil
1 teaspoon thyme
½ cup farmer's cheese

Dissolve yeast in ½ cup warm water (85 °F) for 8 minutes without stirring. Add oil, honey, and salt. Beat egg and add half. Knead dough with as much flour as it will take to give it a proper elasticity. Let dough rise for 1 hour in a warm (about 80 °F) place. Prepare filling:

Finely chop mushrooms and onion. Sauté in oil and thyme. Simmer until all liquid has evaporated. When vegetables have cooled, stir in the cheese, adding a pinch of salt if desired.

Roll out dough and make about 20 "cookies" by cutting with a glass or round cookie cutter. Put 1 tablespoon of filling on each. Moisten edges with beaten egg and fold over, pressing edges together with a fork.

Put uszkis on a greased baking sheet. Brush with remaining beaten egg and bake in oven, preheated to 390 °F, for about 15 minutes, until golden.

Uszkis are traditionally served with Russian borsch, but go well with all soups. They may also be used as a first course, served with a salad. They freeze well.

STUFFED TOMATOES

`4 large beefsteak tomatoes
½ cup brown rice
1 cup water
⅓ cup shelled peas
4 tablespoons olive oil
2 tablespoons herbal vinegar
½ teaspoon crushed rosemary
½ teaspoon crushed mint
4 lettuce leaves

Cut cap off tomatoes and remove pulp.

Cook rice 40 minutes. During the last 5 minutes, add peas. Let cool, then stir in a little tomato juice, olive oil, vinegar, and herbs.

Stuff tomatoes with rice mixture, replace cap, and serve on lettuce leaves.

ZUCCHINI BAKED WITH CHEESE

1 pound zucchini
2 spring onions
1–2 tablespoons thyme
1 cup milk
½ cup grated cheddar cheese

Slice zucchini and put in greased oven-proof dish. Chop onions, cut green tops fine, and sprinkle over zucchini with crushed thyme.

Pour milk over vegetables and sprinkle grated cheese on top. Bake in oven, preheated to 390 °F, for 20 minutes.

WAX BEANS BAKED WITH CHEESE

½ pound wax beans
2 tablespoons butter
⅓ cup grated Parmesan cheese
4 tablespoons cut chives

Boil beans for 6–8 minutes. Remove while still crisp. Drain and put in oven-proof dish. Put butter on top and sprinkle with Parmesan cheese.

Put dish in oven, preheated to 375 °F, until cheese is golden, about 20 minutes.

Serve sprinkled with finely cut chives.

CREAMED WAX BEANS

1 pound wax beans
4 tablespoons butter
1 bunch parsley
2 teaspoons fresh, chopped savory
¾ cup vegetable bouillon
¾ cup milk or cream
1 tablespoon butter
1 tablespoon flour

Boil beans for 1 minute. Drain and pour cold water over beans. Drain again.

Mix beans with melted butter and chopped parsley and savory. Pour boiling bouillon over beans and simmer for 8–10 minutes. Add milk or cream.

Mix softened butter with flour and thicken sauce. Add salt and pepper to taste, if desired.

Snow Peas

Snow peas are thin, crisp peas which are eaten with the pod. Snip off ends and remove strings. These peas can be used uncooked in salads, or sautéed slightly and served as an accompaniment, or they can be a component in mixed courses.

Snow peas contain proteins as well as vitamins B and C.

OLD-FASHIONED SNOW PEAS

1 Chinese cabbage or spring cabbage
Fresh lovage
1 cup water
2 tablespoons butter
½ cup snow peas
½ cup milk
Kuzo

Loosen the cabbage leaves a little and insert 6–8 lovage leaves in between them. Put cabbage in boiling water. Add butter and boil cabbage for 10 minutes. Add peas and boil for a few more minutes.

Remove cabbage from water. Add milk. Thicken with a little kuzo mixed with water.

Cut cabbage and put in the sauce. Add salt and pepper to taste, if desired.

SAUTÉED SNOW PEAS

½ pound snow peas
Oil
1 bunch parsley

Snip off ends of peas and sauté them in oil for 3–4 minutes. Sprinkle with chopped parsley.

SAUCES

CELERIAC SAUCE

1 onion
Oil
1 3½-ounce slice celeriac
2 cups milk/vegetable bouillon
3 tablespoons flour

Chop onion and sauté in oil. Add finely chopped celeriac. Add liquid and bring to a boil.

Thicken sauce with flour mixed with water. Cook for 5–10 minutes, adding salt to taste. You can also add chopped savory or parsley.

SWEET AND SOUR CHIVE SAUCE

1 cup milk
1½ cups vegetable bouillon
1 tablespoon kuzo
Honegar (half honey, half cider vinegar)
4 tablespoons finely cut chives

Bring milk and bouillon to a boil. Mix kuzo with a little water and add to liquid. Add honegar and cut chives to taste. Cook for 4 minutes, adding salt to taste.

LEMON SAUCE

1½ cups milk or vegetable bouillon
Kuzo or cornstarch
Juice of 1 lemon
½ cup whipping cream

Bring milk or bouillon to a boil. Mix kuzo or cornstarch with water and beat it into the liquid. Cook sauce for 5 minutes, adding lemon juice, and salt and pepper to taste.

Whip the cream until stiff and fold into the sauce before serving.

SAUCE A LA PROVENCE

1¼ cups sour cream or crème fraîche
1 egg yolk (may be omitted)
4 tablespoons lemon juice
2 tablespoons olive oil
½ cup watercress
1 small bunch of chives
2 tablespoons chopped chervil or
   parsley

Beat together all the ingredients, or put them in a blender. Add a little pressed garlic, and salt and pepper to taste.

COTTAGE CHEESE SAUCE

1 cup cottage cheese
1 cup milk
1 clove garlic
1 bunch parsley

Stir cottage cheese with milk until smooth. Add pressed garlic and chopped parsley and salt and pepper to taste.

ITALIAN SAUCE

1½ cups mushrooms
2 shallots
½ lemon
½ cup sunflower oil
1 bay leaf
2 cloves
1 tablespoon chopped parsley
½ cup apple cider
½ cup whipping cream

Chop shallots and mushrooms fine. Remove the peel, then cut lemon in thin slices.

Heat sunflower oil, add mushrooms, onions, lemon slices, bay leaf, and cloves. Simmer for 5 minutes; add parsley, apple cider, and whipping cream. Cook sauce over low heat until it thickens.

Remove lemon slices, cloves, and bay leaf. Add salt and pepper to taste.

SPAGHETTI SAUCE

1 onion
1 green pepper
2 cups mushrooms
4 tablespoons oil
1 tablespoon fresh, chopped oregano
4 tablespoons chopped parsley
4 tablespoons finely cut chives
3 tablespoons flour
2 cups milk or vegetable bouillon
4 tablespoons grated Parmesan cheese
4 tablespoons tomato paste

Chop onion, pepper, and mushrooms fine and cook in oil until onion is translucent. Add herbs. Thicken with flour mixed with milk or vegetable bouillon.

Cook sauce for 5 minutes. Add grated cheese and tomato paste and salt and pepper to taste.

GRAPE SAUCE

½ pound grapes
2 tablespoons butter
¼ cup pumpkin seeds
¾ cup sour cream or crème fraîche

Cut grapes in half and remove seeds, if any. Stir grapes and pumpkin seeds in melted butter for 5 minutes. Add sour cream or crème fraîche and heat. Add salt and pepper to taste.

Grape sauce is very tasty with pâtés such as almond pâté or cold herb pâté.

PIQUANT SAUCE

1 onion
4 tablespoons butter
3 tablespoons herbal vinegar
1 stem of parsley
1 stem of thyme
2 bay leaves
2 cups vegetable bouillon
1 tablespoon honey
1 tablespoon chopped capers
2 tablespoons chopped pickled
  cucumber
Cornstarch or kuzo

Chop onion fine and sauté in butter until translucent. Add herbal vinegar, herbs, bay leaves, bouillon, and honey. Let simmer over low heat for 15 minutes. Add finely chopped capers and pickled cucumber. Thicken sauce. Add salt to taste, if desired.

DIPS

MUSHROOM DIP

1½ cups mushrooms
1 shallot
2 tablespoons oil
1 tablespoon lemon juice
½ clove of garlic
½ cup sour cream (18% fat content)
  or crème fraîche
½ cup cottage cheese
2 tablespoons fresh, chopped herbs

Chop mushrooms and shallot fine. Sauté in oil together with lemon juice and pressed garlic. Let simmer until most of the liquid has evaporated. Cool.

Stir together sour cream or crème fraîche and cottage cheese until smooth. Add the cooled mushrooms, chopped herbs, and salt and pepper to taste.

DILL DIP

1 cup ymer* or yogurt
2 tablespoons tahini
1 bunch dill

Stir ymer or yogurt with tahini and finely chopped dill. Add salt and pepper to taste, if desired.

*This is a sour milk product, much used in Denmark.

CHUTNEY DIP

1 cup sour cream or crème fraîche
½ teaspoon tamari
1–2 tablespoons chopped mango
  chutney
2 tablespoons finely chopped coconut

Add tamari and mango chutney to sour cream to taste, then add coconut.

Other dips may be made from ymer, yogurt, or sour cream, to which you add chopped herbs, pressed garlic, chopped olives, pickled cucumbers, or capers.

AVOCADO CREAM

2 ripe avocados
¼–½ cup sour cream or crème fraîche
1 small shallot
2 tablespoons chopped pickled
  cucumber
2 tablespoons dill

Halve avocados, remove meat, and mash. Mix with sour cream until smooth. Add finely chopped shallot to avocado together with very finely chopped pickled cucumber and dill. Add salt and pepper to taste, if desired.

DESSERTS

Fresh fruit rounds out any meal very well. The carbohydrates are broken down slowly in the body, and fruit contains vitamins A, B, and C in varying quantities, plus minerals and trace minerals such as calcium, iron, phosphorus, manganese, zinc, and copper.

Fruit should be eaten unpeeled if possible, since the peel is an excellent source of fiber.

Cheeses and whole grain breads may also be used as desserts, but they contain substantially more calories than fresh fruit.

Sweet desserts are served infrequently in a health-conscious household, but a dessert sweetened with honey or unrefined sugar now and then would hardly harm healthy people.

PINEAPPLE PIE

6 tablespoons butter
1 cup all-purpose flour
2 tablespoons cold water
1 egg yolk
1 teaspoon baking powder
½ pineapple
2 tablespoons honey
1 cup farmer's cheese
2 tablespoons chopped nuts

Mix butter and flour. Add water, egg yolk, and baking powder. Mix dough briefly. Place in cool area for 30 minutes.

Roll dough out and put in a greased 10-inch pie pan. Prick dough with fork. Bake for 15–20 minutes, until light brown, in an oven preheated to 390 °F.

Slice and peel pineapple. Squeeze a couple of slices to make about ½ cup liquid. Heat pineapple juice with honey, then stir it in the cheese. Add more honey, if desired.

Let crust cool. Spoon cheese on it. Cut pineapple into small pieces and sprinkle on top.

Sprinkle with chopped nuts.

Let the pie sit for a couple of hours before serving.

ORANGE MOUSSE

2 eggs, separated
4 tablespoons unrefined sugar
Juice from 4 oranges
3 teaspoons agar-agar
1 cup whipping cream

Beat egg yolks well with sugar.

Bring unstrained orange juice to a boil. Mix agar-agar with water and add to orange juice. Cook for a couple of minutes. Remove pan from heat. When juice has cooled a little, beat in the egg yolk and sugar. Remember that agar-agar stiffens rather quickly.

Separately, whip egg whites and cream until stiff. Fold carefully into the thickened juice.

Place mousse in refrigerator for a couple of hours. You can top with orange or tangerine wedges.

CELERY WITH CHEESE FILLING

4–8 stalks of celery
2 ounces cream cheese
2 ounces Danablue cheese
4 tablespoons cream
1 shallot

Cut celery in short pieces. Mix the two kinds of cheese with cream and finely chopped shallot until smooth.

Put cheese mixture on celery pieces. You can serve radishes or grapes with these.

CELERY WITH PINEAPPLE FILLING

4–8 stalks of celery
2 ounces cream cheese
2–3 slices of pineapple
10 black, pitted olives

Cut celery in pieces. Stir together softened cheese and pineapple cut into tiny pieces. Put mixture on celery pieces. Garnish with halved olives.

HONEYDEW WITH GRAPES

Quarter a honeydew melon and remove seeds. Halve grapes and remove seeds. Garnish the honeydew, in individual servings, with grape halves and almond slivers.

Honeydew melon can be served with other fresh fruits such as raspberries.

CARROT CAKE

½ pound fresh carrots
1 medium-size potato, cooked
2 eggs
4 tablespoons honey
1 tablespoon oil
⅓ cup chopped nuts
⅓ cup chopped dates
⅓ cup raisins
1 teaspoon ground cinnamon
1 teaspoon crushed cloves
½ teaspoon ground nutmeg
½ cup whole wheat flour
½ cup all-purpose flour
1½ teaspoons baking powder

Grate carrots and potato fine. Stir in eggs and add honey, oil, chopped nuts, dates, raisins, and the spices.

Add flour and baking powder. Stir well. Pour batter into a greased cake pan.

Bake in oven, preheated to 390 °F, for 35 minutes.

MIXED FRUIT COMPOTE

1 cup mixed dried fruit
2 cups water

Soak dried fruit for 6–8 hours. Cut in small pieces and cook in the same water for 15–20 minutes, or until most of the water has evaporated and the compote has thickened.

Serve the compote with toasted slivered almonds and milk or sour cream.

BAKED BANANAS WITH RASPBERRIES

4 bananas
1 pint raspberries

Put bananas in oven, preheated to 390 °F, for 8–10 minutes. Peel the bananas and spoon raspberries over them.

Cook the raspberries with a little water and honey if you want a warm sauce.

GLAZED NUT CAKE

½ cup whole wheat flour
½ cup all-purpose flour
1 teaspoon baking powder
1 pinch salt
1 pinch ground nutmeg
⅓ cup nuts
4 tablespoons honey
½ cup orange yogurt
2 tablespoons butter

Mix together the flour with baking powder, salt, and ground nutmeg. Coarsely chop ¾ of the nuts and add to flour mixture.

Blend 3 tablespoons honey with yogurt. Stir into flour. It may be necessary to add a little more yogurt, as dough should be neither too stiff nor too soft.

Roll out dough and put in a greased cake pan. Bake in oven, preheated to 375 °F, for about 20 minutes.

Glaze cake 5 minutes before it is done. Mix melted butter and 1 tablespoon honey. Chop remainder of the nuts and add to glaze. Spread glaze over cake. Return to oven for another 5 minutes.

NECTARINE SALAD

3 nectarines
8–10 prunes
8–10 green plums
½ cup sour cream or crème fraîche
2 tablespoons chopped almonds

Cube nectarines. Halve prunes and plums and mix with nectarine cubes. Divide fruits into 4 dessert glasses and top with sour cream and chopped almonds.

CHEESE-FRUIT SALAD

5 ounces cheddar cheese
½ pound blue grapes
2 kiwi fruits
2–4 slices pineapple
2 tablespoons chopped nuts
Alfalfa sprouts

Cube cheese, halve grapes, and remove seeds. Peel and slice kiwi fruits. Cut kiwi slices in half. Peel pineapple and cut in small pieces.

Mix cheese cubes and fruits. Serve in dessert glasses. Sprinkle with nuts and sprouts.

NUT TART

⅔ cup whole wheat flour
⅓ cup all-purpose flour
½ cup butter
1 egg, separated
2–3 tablespoons orange juice
2 tablespoons unrefined sugar
⅔ cup nuts
¼ cup orange juice

Mix the flour with butter, egg yolk, orange juice, and sugar. Roll out dough and put in pie pan.

Whip egg white with sugar until stiff. Chop nuts and fold in egg white together with orange juice.

Put nut mixture in pie and bake in oven, preheated to 390°F, for 25–30 minutes.

KIWI SALAD

2–3 pears
2 tablespoons orange juice
½ pound green grapes
2 kiwi fruits
½ cup whipping cream
2 tablespoons chopped walnuts

Dice pears and stir in orange juice. Halve grapes, remove seeds. Peel and slice kiwi fruits. Mix fruits and divide into 4 dessert glasses. Top with stiffly whipped cream and sprinkle with chopped walnuts.

GORGONZOLA PEARS

2 large ripe pears
4 ounces Gorgonzola cheese, sliced
⅓ cup slivered almonds

Peel and halve pears. Remove cores. Put pear halves, cut side down, in an oven-proof dish.

Put sliced cheese on pears. Sprinkle with almond slivers and put in oven, preheated to 390°F, for 15 minutes.

MIXED PEAR SALAD

1–2 oranges
2 avocados
2 pears
⅓ cup pistachios, or other nuts

Peel and divide oranges. Cut sections lengthwise.

Peel and slice avocados and pears. Cover slices with orange juice to prevent browning.

Put orange, avocado, and pear slices alternately on a round dish. Sprinkle with chopped pistachios or other nuts.

CHEESE PEARS

2 large ripe pears
1¾ ounces blue cheese
4–5 tablespoons cream
2 tablespoons chopped walnuts

Halve pears lengthwise and core.

Stir cheese with cream until smooth. Fill pears with cheese mixture and sprinkle with chopped walnuts.

BAKED PEARS

6 tablespoons butter
¾ cup all-purpose flour
2 tablespoons unrefined sugar
1 egg
2 tablespoons chopped dates
3 tablespoons finely chopped nuts
2 tablespoons cream
4 firm pears

Mix butter, flour, and sugar. Beat egg and add half to dough. Knead well and put dough in a cool place while preparing the filling.

Mix chopped dates and nuts with cream. Peel pears and remove cores.

Roll out dough into 4 circles. Place 1 pear on each circle and add filling. Fold dough over pears and press edges together.

Brush dough with the rest of egg and bake 35 minutes, until golden, in oven preheated to 390 °F.

ALMOND-APPLE CAKE

1 ½ pounds sweet apples
⅓ cup almonds
2 egg whites
¼ cup sour cream or crème fraîche
½ cup granola or breadcrumbs
Honey or unrefined sugar

Peel and cut apples into wedges. Steam until half done in a minimum of water. Put wedges in ovenproof dish.

Chop half of the almonds fine, the other half coarse. Whip egg whites until almost stiff and blend with chopped almonds, sour cream, and granola or breadcrumbs. Add honey or sugar for a sweeter cake.

Spoon almond mixture over apples and put dish in oven, preheated to 390 °F, until surface is golden, about 30 minutes.

UPSIDE-DOWN APPLE CAKE

2 tablespoons butter
4 tablespoons unrefined sugar
1 pound sweet apples
⅓ cup halved walnuts
5 tablespoons butter
¼ cup unrefined sugar
2 eggs
¾ cup all-purpose flour
¼ cup plus 1 tablespoon buckwheat
  flour
1 teaspoon baking powder
3 tablespoons lemon juice

Line circular mold with foil.

Melt 2 tablespoons butter and 4 tablespoons sugar and pour mixture into the mold. Peel apples and cut into wedges. Put in mold, alternating with halved walnuts.

Stir 5 tablespoons butter and ¼ cup sugar together until soft. Beat in the eggs, one at a time. Add sifted flour and baking powder. Stir and add lemon juice.

Pour batter over apples in mold. Place on bottom of oven and bake at 390 °F, for 50–60 minutes.

When cake has cooled, turn it upside down and remove it from mold. The apple-walnut part will be on top.

APPLE TART

4 tablespoons butter
4 tablespoons unrefined sugar
Vanilla
1 egg
⅓ cup chopped nuts
¼ cup plus 1 tablespoon all-purpose
  flour
1 teaspoon baking powder
1 egg white
4 tablespoons chopped dates
1 pound sweet apples

Cream butter with sugar and vanilla until smooth. Stir in a whole egg and chopped nuts. Add sifted flour and baking powder. Whip egg white until stiff and fold carefully into the batter.

Put batter in a greased pie pan. Sprinkle with dates. Add peeled and sliced apples.

Bake tart in oven, preheated to 375 °F, for 40 minutes.

BAKING

In addition to the ordinary all-purpose flour, the recipes that follow make use of more coarsely ground flour, whole grains, and nuts, to increase the nutritional value of the breads.

Yeast is most often used as a means of leavening the dough. Yeast consists of live cells, which must be care-fully handled. It is important that the liquid in which the yeast is dissolved is the right temperature.

Either active dry yeast or compressed yeast may be used in these recipes. One package of active dry yeast may be substituted for one cake of compressed yeast. If dry yeast is used, it should be dissolved in liquid between 105° and

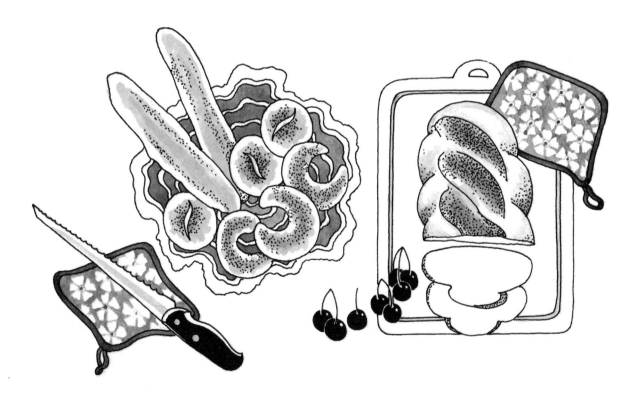

115 °F, without stirring, for 3–5 minutes. If compressed yeast is chosen, it should be dissolved, without stirring, in liquids at 85 °F for 8–10 minutes.

A small amount of carbohydrates, such as honey or sugar, is added to dough in order to further the growth of the yeast. Salt is added to improve the taste and to better the consistency of the baked product. You can better the product even further by adding vitamin C, in the form of a couple of tablespoons of lemon juice.

The dough should be placed in a warm place (77 °–86 °F) to rise.

Only a few of the following recipes call for soaking grain products, but you may use this process with all of them, placing them at room temperature in the required amount of liquid. Save ½ cup to be warmed later and used for dissolving the yeast. If you choose this process, the dough will have a lower temperature and its rising time must be doubled. On the other hand, this process gives the baked product a far better consistency because the grain product has had a chance to absorb the liquid. For further information about this process, see Sesame Rolls.

All the baked products may be frozen. Rye bread (pumpernickel) and white bread may be sliced before freezing. Freeze the products in plastic bags before they have cooled completely. If you freeze them while they are still lukewarm, they will retain their crispness.

Sourdough

Use of sourdough in baking is an old process which is being revived today. The rising is caused by lactic acid, which means that the products are more digestible.

At first glance, it seems difficult to bake with sourdough, but the actual work involved is really not very much. One only has to plan well in advance. Once you have a starter, you can make the dough, and from this take ½ cup of dough each time you bake, keeping this starter in a small container in the refrigerator until the next time you bake. You can also freeze the starter, letting it become active again by leaving it at room temperature for 24 hours.

SOURDOUGH RYE BREAD (PUMPERNICKEL)

Starter:
1 cup whole grain rye flour
2 teaspoons salt
1¼ cups yogurt

Dough:
3¾ cups lukewarm water
1½ teaspoons salt
4¾ cups whole grain rye flour
5 cups cracked rye berries
1¼ cups lukewarm water
Vegetable margarine

Make the starter by mixing rye flour and salt with yogurt. Stir. Leave at room temperature for 3 days. Usually, you can smell when the starter is ready for use. It smells sour.

First day, when starter is ready for use: Mix starter with 3 ¾ cups lukewarm water. Add salt and rye flour. Stir dough well and place in warm place for at least 12 hours.

Second day: Blend the cracked rye berries and 1¼ cups lukewarm water in the dough. Stir well. The dough will not be firm enough to knead.

Grease 2 1¾-quart pans with vegetable margarine.

(The use of margarine is justified since the breads may stick to the pans if any other means of greasing is used.)

Divide dough in half and let rise for at least 5 more hours. Cover pans with damp cloths during this time so the dough does not dry out.

Put pans in oven, preheated to 350 °F. When tops of loaves have browned, cover with foil. After 1½ hours, remove breads from pans, turn off oven, and return the breads to the oven for an additional hour.

SMALL WALNUT BREADS

2½ cups yogurt
½ cup water
¼ cup corn oil
2 packages active dry yeast
1 tablespoon salt
1 tablespoon honey
½ cup rye flour
1⅓ cups all-purpose flour
⅓ cup chopped walnuts
½ cup cracked rye
3½–4 cups whole grain rye flour

Mix yogurt, water, and oil. Heat until 105°–115°F, then dissolve yeast in mixture. Let stand for 3–5 minutes, then stir.

Add salt, honey, flour, chopped walnuts, and cracked rye. Stir dough, then add as much rye flour as dough will take. Knead dough until it is smooth and elastic. Allow to rise in a warm place for 1½ hours.

Punch down the dough and divide into 6 small greased aluminum pans. Let rise again for half an hour.

Brush tops with water and bake in oven, preheated to 390°F, for 1 hour.

GRAHAM BREAD

2½ cups skimmed milk
1 cup yogurt
2 packages of active dry yeast
1 tablespoon honey
2 tablespoons oil
2 teaspoons salt
½ cup wheat germ
½ cup plus 2 tablespoons buckwheat
  flour
3½ cups whole wheat flour
2–2¼ cups all-purpose flour

Heat milk and yogurt to 105°–115°F. Dissolve yeast in mixture; let stand for 3–5 minutes.

Add honey, oil, salt, wheat germ, buckwheat flour, and whole wheat flour. Stir well. Knead in the all-purpose flour, a little at a time. Knead dough thoroughly and let rise in a warm place for 1 hour.

Punch down dough and knead again. Put dough in 2 greased bread pans and let rise again for 30 minutes.

Brush tops with oil and bake in oven, preheated to 390°F, for 35–40 minutes. Remove breads from pans, turn off oven, and return breads for 10 minutes longer.

You can also make rolls or small French breads from this dough, in which case, only bake for about 25 minutes.

KAMMA'S RYE BREAD

¾ cup cracked rye berries
¼ cup linseeds
2 cups boiling water
1¼ cups buttermilk
1 cup water
2 packages active dry yeast
1 tablespoon honey
1½ teaspoons salt
Juice from ½ lemon
4 tablespoons oil
6 cups rye flour
1½ cups all-purpose flour

Soak cracked rye and linseeds in 2 cups boiling water overnight.

Heat buttermilk with 1 cup water until it reaches 105°–115°F. Dissolve yeast in mixture and let stand for 3–5 minutes. Pour liquid into the cracked rye, add honey, salt, lemon juice, oil, and rye flour. Knead dough well, adding as much all-purpose flour as it will take.

Put dough to rise in a warm place for 1½ hours. Knead again and divide into 3 greased pans. Allow to rise again for 1 hour.

Prick breads with fork and brush with water. Bake in oven, preheated to 390°F, for 1¼ hours.

SPICED COTTAGE CHEESE BREAD

⅓ cup whole wheat berries
1 package active dry yeast
¼ cup water
¼ pound cottage cheese
2 teaspoons honey
3 tablespoons oil
1 teaspoon salt
1 egg
¼ cup sesame seeds
2 tablespoons chopped parsley
1 tablespoon fresh, chopped sage
3 cups all-purpose flour

Soak wheat berries overnight.

Dissolve yeast in water heated to 105°–115°F, let stand for 3–5 minutes. Add cottage cheese, honey, oil, salt, egg, sesame seeds, chopped herbs, and drained wheat berries.

Mix and add flour, a little at a time, as much as dough will take. Knead, then let rise in a warm place for 2 hours.

Punch down dough and knead lightly. Put in a greased baking pan, or shape into rolls or small French breads. Let rise again for 30 minutes, then brush with oil or melted butter.

Bake for 25 minutes in a 390°F oven. If you are baking breads, remove from pans after 25 minutes and bake for 15 minutes longer.

ROSEMARY BREAD

½ cup cracked wheat
½ cup sesame seeds
½ cup wheat bran
2½ cups yogurt
2 packages active dry yeast
¼ cup corn oil
1½ teaspoons honey
2 teaspoons salt
1 tablespoon crushed rosemary
1⅓ cups whole wheat flour
2¼ cups all-purpose flour
1 cup rye flour

Soak cracked wheat, sesame seeds, and wheat bran in yogurt for 12 hours, then heat to 105°–115°F.

Dissolve yeast in the yogurt and let stand for 3–5 minutes. Add oil, honey, salt, crushed rosemary, and whole wheat and rye flours.

Knead dough, adding all-purpose flour until dough is smooth and elastic. Knead thoroughly and set to rise in a warm place for 1 hour.

Punch down dough and knead again. Shape into 24 oblong buns.

Let buns rise again for 30 minutes, brush them with oil, and bake in oven, preheated to 390°F, for 30 minutes.

CARAWAY FLUTES (FRENCH BREADS)

2 packages active dry yeast
3 cups lukewarm water
½ cup cracked wheat berries
½ cup wheat germ
¼ cup plus 2 tablespoons soy flour
1 tablespoon honey
1½ teaspoons salt
1–2 tablespoons caraway seeds
1⅔ cups whole wheat flour
3 cups all-purpose flour

Dissolve yeast in 105°–115°F water, let stand for 3–5 minutes. Stir in cracked wheat, wheat germ, soy flour, honey, salt, and caraway seeds. Add whole wheat flour. Mix dough with as much all-purpose flour as it takes for the dough to separate from sides of bowl. Mix dough, but do not knead.

Set dough to rise in a warm place for 1 hour. Knead dough with a little more all-purpose flour, until it comes off fingers easily. Shape into 6 French breads, 16 inches long. Put French breads on a greased cookie sheet and let rise again for 30 minutes.

Brush breads with water and bake in oven, preheated to 480°F, for 15–20 minutes. A bowl of water can be placed at the bottom of the oven if crisper bread is desired.

OLD HANSEN'S FRENCH BREAD

4¼ cups all-purpose flour
1⅔ cups whole wheat flour
1 cup sesame seeds
3 cups water
2 packages active dry yeast
1 tablespoon honey
1½ teaspoons salt
2 tablespoons oil
½ cup all-purpose flour
Cold coffee

Combine flours and sesame seeds in a bowl and beat well with a beater, adding air to mixture.

Heat water to 105°–115°F and pour the yeast in; let stand for 3–5 minutes. Add to flour, honey, salt, and oil.

Stir dough well with a spoon, adding extra flour if dough is too thin. Do not knead.

Put bowl into an airtight plastic bag (leave room for the dough to rise) and allow dough to rise in a warm place for 1 hour.

Spread out the last ½ cup of flour on the counter. Put dough on top of the flour, folding dough up repeatedly until it is elastic and has a suitable consistency.

Shape 24 French breads 6 inches long, and put on a greased cookie sheet. Let rise for 30 minutes.

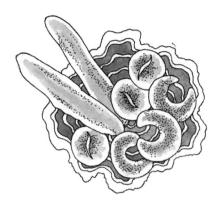

Score French breads with a knife and brush with cold coffee. Bake in oven, preheated to 435°F, for 20 minutes. The crust will be crisper if you put a bowl of water at the bottom of the oven while baking.

OATMEAL BREAD

1 cup oats
1⅓ cups whole wheat flour
3 cups water
2 packages active dry yeast
1½ cups milk
3 tablespoons honey
2 tablespoons lemon juice
1½ teaspoons salt
4 tablespoons oil
⅔ cup barley flour
⅓ cup chopped walnuts
3¾ cups all-purpose flour

Oatmeal breads are very delicious. Oats, wheat, and barley are a tasty combination, and walnuts go well with it.

Pour water over oats, mixed with whole wheat flour. Let stand for a couple of hours, or until next day.

Dissolve yeast in milk heated to 105°–115°F, let stand 3–5 minutes, then mix with oats and flour. Add honey, lemon juice, salt, oil, barley flour, and chopped walnuts. Add 3 cups of the all-purpose flour and mix in thoroughly. This dough does not require kneading. Let rise, uncovered, in a warm place for 2 hours.

Knead dough until smooth, adding the rest of the all-purpose flour. Do not let the dough become too stiff.

Put dough either in 2 oiled bread pans, or shape into 36–38 rolls or small French breads. Let rise again for 1 hour, then brush tops with oil or beaten egg.

Bake in oven, preheated to 390°F. The rolls should bake for 30 minutes, the 2 breads for 40–45 minutes. Remove from pans, turn off heat, and return to oven for another 10 minutes.

FOUR-GRAIN BREAD

⅓ cup cracked oats
⅓ cup cracked wheat
⅓ cup cracked rye
⅓ cup cracked barley
2½ cups boiling water
2 packages active dry yeast
½ cup water
¾ cup yogurt
1 tablespoon honey
1 tablespoon salt
2 tablespoons lemon juice
¼ cup sunflower oil
2⅓ cups whole wheat flour
4½ cups all-purpose flour

Pour water over cracked grains and let soak for 12 hours.

Dissolve yeast in water heated to 105°–115°F, let stand for 3–5 minutes, then add to softened grains with yogurt, honey, salt, lemon juice, oil, and whole wheat flour. Stir in the all-purpose flour, a little at a time. When dough separates from sides, remove and knead thoroughly.

Put dough to rise in a warm place for 1½–2 hours. It should double in size.

Knead dough lightly again, divide and place in 2 greased 6×9 bread pans, or shape into rolls or buns. Let rise again for 30 minutes, then brush tops with oil.

If you make buns or rolls, bake in oven, preheated to 425°F, for 25–30 minutes. If you are making two loaves, preheat oven to 390°F, and bake for 40 minutes. Remove loaves from pans. Turn off oven and return loaves to oven for another 10 minutes.

SESAME ROLLS IN PAN

3½ cups whole wheat flour
½ cup cracked wheat berries
2½ cups warm water
2 packages active dry yeast
½ cup milk
1 tablespoon honey
¼ cup oil
1½ teaspoons salt
1 tablespoon lemon juice
⅓ cup sesame seeds
1 celery stalk
1 egg
About 3¾ cups all-purpose flour

Soak whole wheat flour and cracked wheat in 2½ cups water for at least 12 hours.

Dissolve yeast in milk heated to 105°–115°F, let stand for 3–5 minutes, then add to flour mixture. Add honey, oil, salt, lemon juice, and sesame seeds. Save some of the sesame seeds to sprinkle on top of rolls.

Chop celery very fine and mix in the dough. Mix in half of a beaten egg. Stir in all-purpose flour, a little at a time.

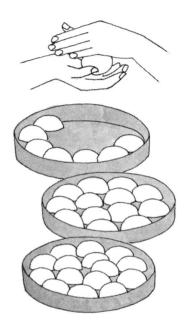

When dough separates from sides, remove and knead it well.

Let dough rise in a warm place for 2 hours. Knead it again and shape into small rolls. Place the rolls close together in 3 greased round, flat pans. Let rise again for 30 minutes.

Brush rolls with remaining beaten egg and sprinkle with sesame seeds. Put rolls in oven, preheated to 435°F, and bake for 20 minutes. Remove the rolls from pans and put back in the oven for 10 minutes longer. You can also make bread, French bread, or rolls out of this yeast dough.

CARAWAY HORNS

1 cup water
½ cup farmer's cheese
1 package active dry yeast
1 teaspoon honey
¼ cup sunflower oil
1 teaspoon salt
1 tablespoon caraway seeds plus a little extra for sprinkling
1 egg
¼ cup rye flour
¾ cup whole wheat flour
2¼ cups all-purpose flour

Heat water and cheese to 105°–115°F. Dissolve yeast in mixture and let stand for 3–5 minutes. Add honey, oil, salt, and caraway seeds.

Beat egg and add half to batter together with the rye and whole wheat flours. Knead in as much all-purpose flour as dough will take. Knead well and let dough rise in a warm place for 1 hour.

Punch down the dough and roll out carefully in thin rectangular pieces. Cut dough into triangles. Roll the triangles into croissants and put on a greased baking sheet. This yields about 20 croissants.

Let croissants rise again for ½ hour, brush with remainder of the beaten egg; sprinkle tops with caraway seeds.

Bake in an oven, preheated to 435°F, for 15–20 minutes.

COARSE DINNER BUNS

2 cups cracked wheat berries
½ cup whole wheat flour
3 cups boiling water
2 cups water
2 packages active dry yeast
1 tablespoon honey
2 teaspoons salt
Juice from ½ lemon
2 tablespoons oil
7½ cups all-purpose flour

Pour boiling water over cracked wheat and whole wheat flour and let soak overnight.

Dissolve yeast in water heated to 105°–115°F, let stand for 8–10 minutes, stir, and add to flour mixture. Add honey, salt, lemon juice, and oil. Work in all-purpose flour, a little at a time. When dough separates from sides, knead it thoroughly. Put dough to rise in a warm place for 1 hour.

Punch down the dough and knead again. Form into about 24 oblong buns or rolls. Put on a greased baking sheet in a warm place and let rise again for ½ hour.

Brush with water and put in oven, preheated to 435°F, for 25 minutes.

SMALL NUT BUNS

2 cups skimmed milk
½ cup yogurt
2 packages active dry yeast
2 tablespoons oil
1 tablespoon honey
2 teaspoons salt
½ cup sesame seeds
⅓ cup ground hazelnuts
2⅓ cups whole wheat flour
3¾ cups all-purpose flour

Heat skimmed milk and yogurt to 105°–115°F, then dissolve the yeast. Let stand 3–5 minutes. Add oil, honey, salt, sesame seeds, and ground nuts. Save a few ground nuts for sprinkling on top.

Stir whole wheat flour into the batter to form dough and knead until smooth adding as much all-purpose flour as it will absorb.

Put dough to rise in a warm place for 1 hour. Knead again lightly and shape into 14 small buns about 5 inches long. Put buns on a greased cookie sheet and let rise again for 30 minutes.

Score tops of buns with a knife, brush with oil, and sprinkle with the remaining ground nuts.

Bake for 20 minutes at 390°F.

SUNFLOWER ROLLS

2 cups milk
1 cup farmer's cheese
2 packages active dry yeast
2 tablespoons oil
1 tablespoon honey
1½ teaspoons salt
⅓ cup sunflower seeds
1⅔ cups whole wheat flour
3 cups all-purpose flour
Oil

Heat milk and farmer's cheese to 105°–115°F. Dissolve yeast in the mixture, let stand for 3–5 minutes.

Stir in oil, honey, salt, chopped sunflower seeds, and whole wheat flour. Mix with as much all-purpose flour as it will take for dough to separate from sides of bowl. Knead dough thoroughly and set to rise in a warm place for 1 hour.

Punch down dough and knead lightly again. Shape it into 26 rolls and put on a greased cookie sheet. Let rise again for 30 minutes. Score tops and brush with oil.

Bake rolls in oven, preheated to 390°F, for 30 minutes.

WHOLE GRAIN ROLLS

1 cup whole grain oats and wheat
¼ cup linseeds
2½ cups water
½ pound farmer's cheese
2 packages active dry yeast
1 tablespoon honey
1½ teaspoons salt
2 tablespoons oil
2 teaspoons crushed thyme
¾ cup rye flour
1½ cups whole wheat flour
4 cups all-purpose flour
Oil

Pour 2½ cups boiling water over grains and linseeds.

When grain mixture has cooled, stir in the cheese. Heat to 105°–115°F, then dissolve yeast in mixture. Let stand for 3–5 minutes.

Stir in the honey, salt, oil, crushed thyme, and rye and whole wheat flours. Knead dough, adding all-purpose flour until dough is smooth and elastic. Set dough to rise in a warm place for 1 hour.

Knead dough lightly again and shape into 32 rolls. Place rolls on a greased baking sheet and let rise again for 30 minutes.

Score tops of the rolls, brush with oil, and bake in oven, preheated to 390°F, for 20–25 minutes.

CHEESE ROLLS

½ cup whole wheat berries
½ cup boiling water
2½ cups water
2 packages active dry yeast
1 tablespoon honey
1½ teaspoons salt
2 tablespoons lemon juice
4 tablespoons oil
1½ cups grated cheddar cheese
⅔ cup rye flour
2 cups whole wheat flour
4¾–5½ cups all-purpose flour
Cream

Pour ½ cup boiling water over the wheat berries and let soak overnight. Heat 2½ cups water to 105°–115°F, dissolve yeast in it, and let stand for 3–5 minutes. Add honey, salt, lemon juice, oil, and grated cheddar cheese, together with the whole wheat and water in which it was soaked. Add the rye and whole wheat flour, then stir in the all-purpose flour, a little at a time.

When dough separates from sides of bowl, remove and knead until it becomes elastic. Set dough to rise in a warm place for 1 hour. Punch down dough and knead again. Form 38–40 rolls, put on greased cookie sheet, and let rise again for 30 minutes. Brush tops with cream, sprinkle with a little grated cheese, if desired.

Bake rolls for 25 minutes at 390°F.

SPICED CHEESE ROLLS

2 packages active dry yeast
2½ cups water
½ pound farmer's cheese
1½ teaspoon honey
1½ teaspoons salt
2 tablespoons lemon juice
4 tablespoons oil
2 tablespoons crushed basil
1⅓ cups cracked wheat berries
3⅓ cups whole wheat flour
3½ cups all-purpose flour
5¼ ounces Emmenthal cheese
Cold coffee

Dissolve yeast in 105°–115°F water, let stand for 3–5 minutes. Stir in farmer's cheese, honey, salt, lemon juice, oil, basil, cracked wheat berries, and whole wheat flour. Knead in the all-purpose flour, a little at a time. Knead dough thoroughly and set to rise in a warm place for 1 hour.

Slice the cheese. Put dough on a board sprinkled with flour. Pat dough into a rectangle. Put cheese slices on half of the dough, then fold the other half over, pressing edges lightly together. Cut 24 rolls out of this dough, using a glass. The remaining dough can be shaped into rolls by hand. Put the rolls on a greased cookie sheet and let rise for another 30 minutes.

Brush rolls with cold coffee and bake in oven, preheated to 390°F, for 20–25 minutes.

INDEX

A

Accompaniments, 136
  recipes, 137–54
Acid-alkaline balance, 4
Agar-agar, 14–15
Algae, 14–15
African vegetables with couscous, 88
Almond(s), 12. *See also* Nut(s)
  -apple cake, 164
  cream, avocado with, 70
  dip, artichokes with, 69
  pâté, 134
  potatoes, 91
  -raisin sauce, Brussels sprouts in, 148
  soup, 64
Amino acids, 1–2. *See also* Protein(s)
  in grains, 7
  in legumes, 5
Appetizers. *See* First courses
Apple cake, upside-down, 165
Apple tart, 165
Arame, 14
Arrowroot. *See* Kuzo
Arthritis, 4
Artichoke(s), 81
  with almond dip, 69
  au gratin, 81
  with egg filling, 82
  with garlic dip, 69
  hearts with creamed spinach, 68
  hearts with lentil purée, 68
Asparagus
  with cheese sauce, 69
  -potatoes, 82

Aubergine(s), 82
  au gratin, 83
  with bean filling, 83
  with rice stuffing, 84
  salad, Greek eggplant, 130
  sautéed, with herbs, 141
Autumn casserole, 94
Avocado
  with almond cream, 70
  cream, 158
  cream, cauliflower with, 141
  cream, with cheese puffs, 135
  cream, kohlrabi with, 72
  ginger, 70
  olive, 70
  salad, 37
  soup, -cheese, 55
  soup, Mexican, 54
  soup, Spanish, 55
Azuki beans, 6–7. *See also* Bean(s), dried

B

Baked baby beets, 101
Baked bananas with raspberries, 161
Baked bean loaf, 122
Baked beans, 139
Baked beets I, 101
Baked beets II, 150
Baked Brussels sprouts with cheese, 148
Baked carrots, 144
Baked chestnuts with cheese, 93
Baked cottage cheese dish, 91
Baked fennel, 142

Baked fettucine, 140
Baked macaroni, 139
Baked olive potatoes, 146
Baked onions, 148
Baked pancakes with cheese, 130
Baked parsnips, 148
Baked pears, 164
Baked potatoes with cheese, 146
Baked potatoes with parsley root, 145
Baked rice, 137
Baked sesame potatoes, 146
Baked sweet potatoes with pineapple, 146
Baked sweet potatoes with raisins, 146
Baking, 166–7
Banana(s)
  baked with raspberries, 161
  Indian casserole with curried, 117
  rice with baked, 115
  salad, 38
Barley, 9
  whole, 138
Bean(s), dried, 5–7. *See also* specific beans;
    Sprout(ing)(s)
  baked, 139
  casserole, Italian, 129
  loaf, baked, 122
  pâté, 119
  in a pot, 84
  salad, Italian, 134
  salad, spiced, 71
Bean(s), green
  filling, aubergines with, 83
  nutty, 128
  salad, haricots verts, 40

Bean(s), green (*continued*)
 salad, Indian, 40
Bean sprout salad, 40
Bean(s), wax
 baked, with cheese, 153
 creamed, 153
 with olives, 79
Beets
 baked I, 101
 baked II, 150
 baked baby, 101
 in garlic sauce, 150
 horseradish, 47
 overture, 77
 Russian, 77
 salad, mixed, 47
 salad, red and white, 46
 sandwich casserole, 102
 stuffed, with dill sauce, 77
 sweet and sour, 100
 with yogurt dressing, 101
Belgium endive(s)
 au gratin, 73
 salad, 43
 salad, green, 43
 soup, 49
Berg, Dr. Ragner, 4
Bircher-Benner, Dr., 35
Black-eyed peas, 6. *See also* Bean(s), dried
Blended broccoli soup, 56
Blood sugar, 2–3
Bouquet garni, 17
Braised carrots with apples, 144
Braised Chinese cabbage, 147
Braised kohlrabi, 147
Brazil nuts, 12. *See also* Nut(s)
Breads, 166–72
Breakfast, 29
 recipes, 30–31
Broad beans, 7. *See also* Bean(s), dried

Broccoli soup, blended, 56
Brussels sprouts
 in almond raisin sauce, 148
 baked, with cheese, 149
 mousse, 76
 salad, 46
 sauce, fettucine with, 89
 soup, 65
 stewed, with nuts, 149
 in tomato sauce, 149
Buckwheat, 10
 whole, 138
Buffets, 133
Bulgur, 9
Buns, 173
Butter-fried mushrooms, 71

C

Cabbage. *See also* Cabbage, Red
 braised Chinese, 147
 in cole slaw, 42
 Indian curried, 116
 rolls in curry sauce, Indian, 114
 salad, 42
 soup, 58
 soup, light green, 57
 soup, Russian, 58
 spring, steamed in butter, 151
 stewed spring, 151
 stuffed, leaves a la harlekin, 90
 stuffed, leaves with chestnut filling, 94
 stuffed, spring, 104
 walnut, 42
Cabbage, Red. *See also* Cabbage
 salad, with celery, 47
 salad, with kiwi, 48
 salad, with mandarins, 47
 spiced, 151
Cake(s)
 almond-apple, 164

Cake(s) (*continued*)
 almond layer, 126
 carrot, 161
 cherry, 128
 glazed nut, 162
 upside-down apple, 165
Cane syrup, 16
Cannelloni, 85
 delicious cheese, 86
 Venetian, 85
Caramel peaches, 131
Caraway flutes, 170
Caraway horns, 173
Carbohydrates, 2–3
Carrot(s)
 baked, 144
 braised, with apples, 144
 cake, 161
 creamed, 142
 pâté, 119
 pie, stuffed, 143
 purée, 143
 salad, 41
 salad, sweet, 41
 soup, 57
Cashews, 12. *See also* Nut(s)
Casserole(s)
 autumn, 94
 beet sandwich, 102
 with curried bananas, Indian, 117
 Italian bean, 129
 lentil, 95
 spinach fettucine, 105
 whole wheat and vegetable, 90
Cauliflower
 with avocado cream, 141
 with olive sauce, 141
 salad, with blue cheese dressing, 38
 salad, mixed, 38
 stewed, 142

Celeriac
  a la wienerschnitzel, 102
  with mushrooms au gratin, 102
  pâté, 120
  Queen Victoria, 103
  with red nut sauce, 103
  salad, 48
  salad, colored, 48
  sauce, 155
  soup, 64
  walnut cakes, 150
Celery
  a la Espagnole, 104
  with cheese filling, 160
  with pineapple filling, 160
  potatoes, 92
  soup, potato-, 61
Cellulose, 3
Cereals. See Breakfast; Grains
Chanterelle soufflé, 91
Chappatis, 140
Cheese(s), 7
  baked Brussels sprouts with, 149
  baked chestnuts with, 93
  baked cottage cheese dish, 91
  baked pancakes with, 130
  baked potatoes with, 146
  bread, spice cottage, 170
  cannelloni, delicious, 86
  Danablue pie, 107
  as dessert, 159
  dressing, 52
  envelopes, French, 74
  filling, celery with, 160
  -fruit salad, 163
  Gorgonzola pears, 163
  Hans Arne's cottage, 73
  pears, 163
  puffs with avocado cream, 135
  rolls, 174
  rolls, spiced, 175

Cheese(s) (continued)
  salad, 46
  salad, -radish, 50
  in sandwiches, 33–34
  sauce, asparagus with, 69
  sauce, cottage, 156
  soup, avocado-, 55
  soup, potato with, 60
  wax beans baked with, 153
  zucchini baked with, 153
Cherry cake, 128
Chervil soup, 63
Chestnuts, 93
  baked, with cheese, 93
  dried, 7
  filling, stuffed cabbage leaves with, 94
  kohlrabi soup with, 62
Chiengmai vegetables, 111
Chinese omelets on rice, 113
Chinese spring rolls, 112
Chinese sweet and sour vegetables, 112
Chinese vegetables, 111
Chioffi, Nancy, 23
Cholesterol, 2
Chutney dip, 158
Coarse dinner buns, 173
Coconuts, 12
Cold creamed vegetable soup, 63
Cold cucumber soup, 54
Cold herb pâté, 132
Cole slaw, 42
Colored celeriac salad, 48
Cooked millet, 138
Cooked rice, 137
Corn, croquettes, 123
Cornmeal, 10
Cornstarch, 10
Cottage cheese sauce, 156
Couscous, 9
  African vegetables with, 88
Cracked wheat, 8

Cream in recipes, 28
Creamed carrots, 143
Creamed wax beans, 153
Crème fraîche (recipe), 37
Creole salad, 87
Crêpes with prune-walnut whip, 132
Croquettes, corn, 122
Croquettes, millet, 123
Cucumber(s)
  soup, cold, 54
  soup, hot, 54
Cumin potatoes, 144
Curry dressing, 52
Curry soup, 59
Cutlets, 118
  lentil-rice, 123

D

Danablue pie, 107
David, Elizabeth, 18
Desserts, 159
  almond layer cake, 126
  caramel peaches, 131
  cherry cake, 128
  crepes with prune-walnut whip, 132
  fruit parfait, 129
  recipes, 160–5
Dill dip, 158
Dips, 158
Doctor's stuffed peppers, 99
Dolmades, Greek, 125

E

Early garden turnip pie, 97
Early garden turnip salad, 50
Early garden turnip salad with curry dressing, 45
Eggplants. See Aubergines
Egg(s), 1, 7

Egg(s) (*continued*)
 Chinese omelets on rice, 113
 -filling, artichokes with, 82
 olive, 79
 substitutes for, 7

F

Fats, 12, 21
 in nuts, 11–12
Fava beans. *See* Broad beans
Fennel
 au gratin, Mads', 86
 baked, 142
 -filled zucchini, 131
 in mushroom sauce, 87
Fettucine with Brussels sprouts sauce, 89
Fiber, 3
First courses, 67
 recipes, 68–79
Florentine spinach, 106
Four-grain bread, 172
French bread(s), 170, 171
French cheese envelopes, 74
French dressing, 51
French lentil salad, 45
French onion pie, 106
French vegetable pie, 127
Fried Jerusalem artichokes, 144
Fried parsnips, 148
Fried pumpkin, 141
Fried rice, 138
Fried tofu, 122
Fructose, 16
Fruit(s), 2
 compote, mixed, 161
 as dessert, 159
 in dessert recipes, 160–5
 dried, 7
 parfait, 129

G

Garbanzo beans, 7. See also Bean(s), dried
 flour from, 10
 in hummus, 34
 salad, 39
Garlic, 18–19
Ginger avocado, 70
Glazed nut cake, 162
Glazed shallots, 148
Gomasio, 7
Gorgonzola pears, 163
Graham bread, 169
Graham flour, 8
Grains, 2, 7–10. *See also* specific grains
Gram flour, 10
Granola, 10
Grapefruit
 salad, 41
 shells, stuffed, 72
Grape sauce, 157
Greek eggplant salad, 130
Greek onions, 148
Green beans. *See* Bean(s), green
Green Belgium endive salad, 43
Green lasagna, 96
Green miso soup, 64
Green pâté, 120
Green potato gratin, 92
Green potato soup, 60
Green spring soup, 56
Green vegetable pie, 89

H

Halvah, 13
Hans Arne's cottage cheese, 72
Haricots, verts, 40
Hazelnuts, 12. *See also* Nut(s)
Herbal dressing, 51
Herbal vinegars, 51

Herb(ed)(s), 17–19
 butter, Jerusalem artichokes with, 150
 pâté, cold
 sautéed eggplant with, 141
 zucchini stuffed with, 109
Hijiki, 15
Honegar, 10
Honey, 16
Hominy grits, 9–10
Honeydew with grapes, 160
Horseradish beets, 47
Hot cucumber soup, 54
Hummus, 34

I

Iceberg lettuce salad, 42
Indian cabbage rolls in curry sauce, 114
Indian casserole with curried bananas, 117
Indian curried cabbage, 116
Indian pilaf, 137
Indian salad, 40
Infections, 4
Ingredients, 5–21. *See also* specific ingredients
Irish soup, 59
Italian bean casserole, 128
Italian bean salad, 134
Italian risotto, 100
Italian sauce, 156
Italian tomato salad, 48
Italian vegetable soup with pesto, 57
Iziki, 14

J

Java pot, 116
Jerusalem artichoke(s)
 fired, 144
 with herb butter, 150
 salad, 43
 soup, 58

K

Kale
  lasagna, 97
  salad, 41
Keeping the Harvest, 23
Kidney beans, 7. *See also* Bean(s), dried
Kiwi salad, 163
Kohlrabi
  with avocado cream, 72
  braised, 147
  pot, 95
  salad, 45
  soup with chestnuts, 62
Kombu, 14
Kruska, 10
Kuzo, 11

L

Lactic acid fermentation, 22–24
Lasagna, 96
  green, 96
  kale, 97
Leek(s)
  au gratin, 76
  pâté, 120
  soup, potato-, 60
  soup, St. Laurentz's, 129
  sweet and sour, 76
  whole grain pancakes with, 100
Legumes, 5–7. *See also* Bean(s), dried
Lemon sauce, 155
Lentils, 5–7. *See also* Bean(s), dried
  casserole, 95
  -nut rissoles, spiced, 121
  purée, artichoke hearts with, 68
  -rice cutlets, 123
  salad, French, 45
  soup, Turkish, 62

Lettuce, salad, iceberg, 42
Light green cabbage soup, 57
Lima beans, 7. *See also* Bean(s), dried
Linseeds, 12
Lunch, 32–34

M

Macaroni tubes, 139
Macrobiotic cooking, 14, 25
Mads' fennel au gratin, 86
Main courses, 80. *See also* Oriental cooking
  recipes, 81–109
Malt extract, 16
Maple syrup, 16
Mead, Gretchen, 23
Menus, 125, 127, 128, 130, 131, 133
Mexican avocado soup, 54
Milk products, 1, 11
  in recipes, 28
  in soups, 53
  substitutions for, 28, 53
Millet, 10
  cooked, 138
  croquettes, 123
Minerals, 3, 5, 7–10, 11, 12, 14, 16, 17
Miso, 11, 22
  soup, green, 64
Mixed beet salad, 47
Mixed cauliflower salad, 38
Mixed fruit compote, 161
Mixed pear salad, 163
Muesli
  Bircher-Benner, 30
  dry, 30
Multicolored potato salad, 44
Multicolored rice salad, 46
Mung beans, 6. *See also* Bean(s), dried;
    Sprout(ing)(s)
  pâté, 121

Mushrooms, 7
  butter-fried, 71
  chanterelle soufflé, 91
  with chives, 40
  cucumbers stuffed with chanterelles, 68
  dip, 158
  pâté, 119
  pie, 133
  salad, 40
  sauce, fennel in, 87
  soup, potato, with, 61
  toast, 71
  zucchini with chaterelles, 108
Mustard, 11

N

National Academy of Sciences, 1
Neopolitan spaghetti, 78
Nectarine salad, 162
Nettle ring, 142
Nettle soup, 56
Nori, 14
Nut(s), 11–12. *See also* specific nuts
  buns, small, 173
  cake, glazed, 162
  filling, zucchini with, 108
  and olive sauce, 132
  rissoles, spiced lentil-, 121
  sauce, celeriac with red, 103
  stewed Brussels sprouts with, 149
  tart, 163
Nutty beans, 128

O

Oatmeal, 30
  bread, 171
Oats, 9, 30
  whole, 138
Okra, 88
Old-fashioned snow peas, 154

Old-fashioned yellow pea soup, 66
Old Hansen's French bread, 171
Olive eggs, 79
Oils, 2, 12, 51
Onion(s), 18
    baked, 148
    glazed shallots, 148
    Greek, 148
    pie, French, 106
    salad, pineapple-, 37
    soup, pink, 62
    stewed spring, 147
    stuffed I, 95
    stuffed II, 147
Orange mousse, 160
Oriental cooking, 110
    recipes, 111-7
Ovo-lacto-vegetarian, 1

P

Pancakes
    a la Provence, 73
    with cheese, baked, 130
    Russian, with spinach in white sauce, 75
    whole grain with leeks, 100
Paranthas, 140
Parisian potatoes, 145
Parsnip(s)
    au gratin, potato and, 93
    baked, 148
    fried, 148
    with green vegetable/walnut stuffing, 98
Pasta, 13-14
    baked macaroni, 139
    baked fettucine, 140
    cannelloni, 85
    delicious cheese cannelloni, 86
    fettucine with Brussels sprouts sauce, 89
    green lasagna, 96
    kale lasagna, 97

Pasta (*continued*)
    macaroni tubes, 139
    Neopolitan spaghetti, 78
    spinach/fettucine casserole, 105
    Venetian cannelloni, 85
Pâté(s), 118
    almond, 134
    bean, 119
    carrot, 119
    celeriac, 120
    cold herb, 132
    green, 120
    leek, 120
    mushroom, 119
    mung bean, 121
    in sandwiches, 32-34
    striped, 126
Peanuts, 12
Pea(s), dried, 5-7. *See also* Bean(s), dried
    soup, old-fashioned yellow, 66
Pea(s), shelled
    salad, 49
    soup, with curry cream, 66
Pepper(s)
    doctor's stuffed, 99
    soup, 65
    stuffed, with tomato sauce, 99
    stuffed, with walnut sauce, 98
Persian rice, 137
Pie(s)
    Danablue, 106
    early garden turnip, 97
    French onion, 106
    French vegetable, 127
    green vegetable, 89
    mushroom, 133
    pineapple, 160
    stuffed carrot, 143
Pineapple-onion salad, 37
Pineapple pie, 160
Pink onion soup, 62

Pinto beans, 7. *See also* Bean(s), dried
Piquant sauce, 157
Pizza, spinach, 105
Porridge
    barley, 30
    buckwheat, 31
    millet, 30
    mixed, 31
    whole grain, 31
Potato(es)
    al la Provence, 145
    almond, 92
    asparagus-, 82
    au gratin, 144
    baked, with cheese, 146
    baked olive, 146
    baked, with parsley root, 145
    baked sesame, 146
    cake, 145
    celery, 92
    cumin, 144
    gratin, green, 92
    mashed, with Swiss chard, 150
    Parisian, 145
    and parsnip au gratin, 93
    salad, 134
    salad with bean sprouts, 44
    salad, multicolored, 44
    salad, tomato, with, 49
    solanine in, 53
    soup, -celery, 61
    soup, with cheese, 50
    soup, green, 60
    soup, -leek, 60
    soup, with mushrooms, 61
Protein(s), 1-2, 5-7, 11
Prune and fig mash, 31
Pumpernickle, 168
Pumpkin, fried, 141
Pumpkin seeds, 12
Purine, 6

Q

Queen Victoria celeriac, 103

R

Radish
  salad, cheese-, 50
  soup, 66
Red and green bean salad, 39
Red and white beet salad, 46
Red avocado salad, 37
Red cabbage. *See* Cabbage, red
Red delesseria, 15
Red seaweed, 15
Rennet, 7
Rice, 9
  baked, 137
  with baked bananas, 115
  Chinese omelets on, 113
  cooked, 137
  cutlets, lentil-, 123
  fried, 138
  Indian pilaf, 137
  in oriental cooking, 110
  Persian, 137
  salad, multicolored, 46
  stuffing, aubergines with, 84
Rissoles, 118
  recipes, 121-3
  in sandwiches, 32-34
  spiced lentil-nut, 121
  wheat, 123
Rolls, 172-5
Rosemary bread, 170
Russian beets, 77
Russian borscht, 55
Russian cabbage soup, 58
Russian pancakes with spinach in white
    sauce, 75

Rye, 9
  bread, Kamma's, 169
  bread, sourdough, 168
  whole, 138

S

Salads, 35-36
  fruit, 162-3
  Greek eggplant, 130
  Italian bean, 134
  potato, 134
  recipes, 37-50
Salad dressing(s), 51
  recipes, 51-52
Salad Nicoise, 39
Salt, 14. *See also* Gomasio; Miso
  in baking, 167
  replacements for, 11, 14
  in sauerkraut, 23-24
Sandwich(es), 33-34
  paste, 34
  spreads, 12-13
Sauce(s), 136
  a la Provence, 156
  recipes, 155-7
Sauerkraut, 23-24
  salad, 48
  soup, 63
Sautéed eggplant with herbs, 141
Sautéed snow peas, 154
Sea lettuce, 15
Seaweed(s), 14-15
  rolls, Seitan, 26
Seeds, 11-12
Seitan, 15, 25-26
Sesame (seeds), 7, 12, 13
  potatoes, baked, 146
  rolls in a pan, 172
Shoyu. *See* Tamari
Side dishes. *See* Accompaniments

Small nut buns, 173
Small walnut breads, 169
Soufflé, chanterelle, 91
Soups, 53
  recipes, 54-66
  St. Laurentz's leek, 129
Sourdough, 167
  rye bread, 168
Soybeans, 6, 10, 11. *See also* Bean(s), dried,
    Miso; Tamari; Tofu
Soy flour, 10
Snow peas, 154
  old-fashioned, 154
  sautéed, 154
Spaghetti sauce, 156
Spanish avocado soup, 55
Spiced bean salad, 71
Spiced cheese balls, 175
Spiced cottage cheese bread, 170
Spiced lentil-nut rissoles, 121
Spiced red cabbage, 151
Spices, 18
Spinach
  creamed, artichoke hearts with, 68
  /fettucine casserole, 105
  -filled zucchini, 107
  Florentine, 106
  pizza, 105
  in white sauce, Russian pancakes with,
    75
Sprout(ing)(s), 20-21
  bean, 6
  salad, bean, 40
  salad, potato, with, 44
Spring cabbage steamed in butter, 151
Spring rolls, Chinese, 112
Spring salad, 41
Squash. *See* Zucchini
Steamed Brussels sprouts with nuts, 149
Stewed cauliflower, 142
Stewed spring cabbage, 151

Stewed spring onions, 147
St. Laurentz's leek soup, 129
Striped pâté, 126
Stuffed Arabic pocket bread (pita), 75
Stuffed beets with dill sauce, 77
Stuffed bread, 152
Stuffed cabbage leaves a la harlekin, 90
Stuffed grapefruit shells, 72
Stuffed onions I, 95
Stuffed onions II, 147
Stuffed peppers with tomato sauce, 99
Stuffed peppers with walnut sauce, 98
Stuffed spring cabbage, 104
Stuffed tomatoes, 153
Stuffed vine leaves, 125
Sugar(s) 2–3, 16. See also Sweeteners
Sunflower rolls, 174
Sunflower seeds, 12
Sunshine bread, 78
Sweet carrot salad, 41
Sweet and sour beets, 100
Sweet and sour chive sauce, 155
Sweet and sour leeks, 76
Sweeteners, 16
Sweet potatoes, 114
    baked, with pineapple, 146
    baked, with raisins, 146
    in spicy sauce, 114
Sweet tangle, 13
Swiss chard with mashed potatoes, 152
Swiss rösti, 145

T

Tahini, 13, 33–34
Tamari, 16
Tofu, 16
    fried, 122
    in sandwiches, 33
Tomato(es)
    with creamed horseradish, 79

Tomato(es) (continued)
    croutons, 78
    salad, Italian, 48
    salad, with potatoes, 49
    sauce, Brussels sprouts in, 149
    sauce, stuffed peppers with, 99
    stuffed, 153
Trace minerals. See Minerals
Turkish lentil soup, 62
Turnip
    pie, early garden, 97
    salad, early garden, 49
    salad, early garden, with curry dressing, 45

U

Underground salad, 44
Upside-down apple cake, 165
Uszki, 152
Utensils, 27

V

Vegetable bouillon, 16, 53
    as a milk substitute, 28, 53
Vegetables, 2–3
    African, with couscous, 88
    a la Grecque, 72
    Bengal, 113
    casserole, whole wheat and, 90
    Chiengmai, 111
    Chinese, 111
    Chinese sweet and sour, 112
    fermented, 22–24
    handling, 28
    pie, French, 127
    pie, green, 89
    in salads, 35–36
    in sandwiches, 33–34
    soup, cold creamed, 63

Vegetables (continued)
    soup, Italian, with presto, 57
    soup, root, 65
    in vegetable bouillon, 53
Vegetarian, 1, 2, 5
Vitamins, 3
    in artichokes, 81
    in cheese, 7
    in eggs, 7
    in fruits, 159
    in grains, 7–10
    in herbs, 17
    in legumes, 6
    in milk products, 11
    in nuts and seeds, 12
    in snow peas, 154
    in sprouts, 21
    in sweeteners, 16
    in sweet potatoes, 114
    in zucchini, 107

W

Wakame, 14
Waldorf salad, 49
Walnut(s), 12
    breads, small, 169
    cabbage, 42
    cakes, celeriac, 150
    sauce, stuffed peppers with, 98
    stuffing, parsnips with green vegetable/, 98
    stuffing, zucchini with, 108
    whip, crêpes with prune-, 132
Wax beans. See Bean(s), wax
Wheat
    bran, 8–9
    flakes, 8
    flour, 8, 9
    rissole, 123

Whole buckwheat, 138
Whole grain pancakes with leeks, 100
Whole grain rolls, 174
Whole grains: barley, oats, rye, 138
Whole meal flakes, 10
Whole wheat, 8
  and vegetable casserole, 90
Wild plants, 19. *See also* Nettle
  in green spring soup, 56

Wild plants (*continued*)
  in salads, 36

Y

Yams. *See* Sweet potatoes
Yeast in baking, 166–7
Yeast extract, 16
Yogurt dressing, 52

Z
Zucchini, 107
  baked with cheese, 153
  with chanterelles, 108
  fennel-filled, 131
  with nut filling, 108
  spinach-filled, 107
  stuffed with herbs, 109
  with walnut stuffing, 108